Promoting Effective Group Work in the Primary Classroom

Promoting Effective Group Work in the Primary Classroom, Second Edition is designed to enhance teachers' and teaching assistants' confidence in engaging their children in effective group work, allowing for more active participation, more on-task focus and higher levels of achievement.

This accessible second edition is packed full of valuable strategies for teachers and fun activities for children, offering guidance on how to create an inclusive and supportive classroom by developing the social, communicative and group working skills of all pupils. It has been thoroughly updated and includes new material on whole school approaches to group work, the risks and challenges involved, and how to involve Teaching Assistants and other support staff in undertaking inclusive and effective group work in classrooms. A tried-and-tested, step-by-step approach encourages both children and their teachers to develop supportive relationships that have been found to facilitate academic performance, positive social behaviour and motivation. Since the first edition, the authors have found that this handbook can be used successfully in many different countries around the world.

With ideas to help resolve problems that might arise and suggested training activities to support pupils, this text is a one-stop resource to ensure effective group work in the classroom. It is an essential guide for both trainee and practising teachers, as well as TAs and support staff, and is a valuable basis for school action.

Ed Baines is Senior Lecturer in Psychology of Education at the UCL Institute of Education, UK.

Peter Blatchford is Professor of Psychology and Education at the UCL Institute of Education, UK.

Peter Kutnick is Emeritus Professor (Psychology of Education) in the Department of Education and Professional Studies at King's College London, UK, as well as Honorary and Visiting Professor at the University of Hong Kong, and Visiting Fellow at Beijing Normal University, China.

TLRP Improving Practice Series

Series Editor: Director of the ESRC Teaching and Learning Programme

Learning How to Learn: Tools for Schools
Mary James *et al.*

Improving Primary Literacy: Linking Home and School
Martin Hughes *et al.*

Improving Primary Mathematics: Linking Home and School (forthcoming)
Martin Hughes *et al.*

Promoting Effective Group Work in the Primary School, 2nd ed
Ed Baines *et al.*

Promoting Effective Group Work in the Primary Classroom

A handbook for teachers
and practitioners

Second Edition

Ed Baines, Peter Blatchford and
Peter Kutnick
with Anne Chowne, Cathy Ota and
Lucia Berdondini

Routledge
Taylor & Francis Group

LONDON AND NEW YORK

Second edition published 2017
by Routledge
2 Park Square, Milton Park, Abingdon, Oxon OX14 4RN

and by Routledge
711 Third Avenue, New York, NY 10017

Routledge is an imprint of the Taylor & Francis Group, an informa business

© 2017 E. Baines, P. Blatchford and P. Kutnick

First published 2009 by Routledge

British Library Cataloguing in Publication Data
A catalogue record for this book is available from the British Library

Library of Congress Cataloging in Publication Data
Names: Baines, Ed, 1969-
Title: Promoting effective group work in the primary classroom : a handbook for teachers and practitioners / Ed Baines, Peter Blatchford and Peter Kutnick with Anne Chowne, Cathy Ota and Lucia Berdondini.
Description: 2nd Edition. | New York : Routledge, 2017.
Identifiers: LCCN 2015051196| ISBN 9781138844421 (Hardback) | ISBN 9781138844438 (Paperback) | ISBN 9781315730363 (Ebook)
Subjects: LCSH: Group work in education–Handbooks, manuals, etc.
Classification: LCC LB1032 .P77 2017 | DDC 371.39/5–dc23
LC record available at http://lccn.loc.gov/2015051196

ISBN: 978-1-138-84442-1 (hbk)
ISBN: 978-1-138-84443-8 (pbk)
ISBN: 978-1-315-73036-3 (ebk)

Typeset in Interstate
by Saxon Graphics Ltd, Derby

Contents

Series preface

The ideas for *Improving Practice* contained in this book are underpinned by high-quality research from the Teaching and Learning Research Programme (TLRP), the UK's largest ever coordinated investment in education enquiry. Each suggestion has been tried and tested with experienced practitioners and has been found to improve learning outcomes - particularly if the underlying principles about Teaching and Learning have been understood. The key, then, remains the exercise of professional judgement, knowledge and skill. We hope that the *Improving Practice* series will encourage and support teachers in exploring new ways of enhancing learning experiences and improving educational outcomes of all sorts.

Acknowledgements

The SPR*in*G (Social Pedagogic Research into Group work) project was a four-year project funded by the Economic and Social Research Council (www.esrc.ac.uk) as part of the Teaching & Learning Research Programme. The production of this handbook for primary schools is the result of a collaborative effort between teachers and researchers based at the Institute of Education, University of Brighton and King's College London.

Contributors

The background research and writing of *Promoting Effective Group Work in the Classroom* was made possible by the collaborative actions of many researchers, teachers, pupils and schools. The authorship of this handbook identifies only the main researchers of the SPRinG project (see Chapter 1) at Key Stages 1 and 2. The ordering of the collaborating authors denotes varying responsibilities in the development, implementation and writing up of the material in the handbook.

Main authors

The names of the main authors are presented alphabetically. This was a truly collaborative effort over many years of working together on various research and education projects.

Ed Baines is currently Senior Lecturer in Psychology of Education at the UCL Institute of Education. He was the principal research officer of the Key Stage 2 component of the SPRinG project and was instrumental in the development of the research. He took a lead role in the conceptualisation and preparation of this handbook, working collaboratively with colleagues and teachers to develop the recommended practices and training activities. Ed is an experienced researcher in this field, working on a range of projects on peer relations and learning in school (funded by the ESRC, Nuffield Foundation, Spencer Foundation and others).

Peter Blatchford is Professor in Psychology and Education at the UCL Institute of Education. He co-directed the SPRinG project and maintained responsibility for the administration of the project in general and the Key Stage 2 developments in particular. Working with Peter Kutnick and Ed Baines, he developed and co-directed projects concerned with social pedagogy and the use of pupil groupings in classrooms that formed the basis of the SPRinG project and the theoretical underpinning of the main principles of effective group working. He has also carried out extensive funded research on class size and the deployment and impact of support staff in schools, as well as break-time and peer relations in schools. He has authored over twelve books and has published over eighty peer-reviewed journal papers on these areas.

Peter Kutnick is Emeritus Professor (Psychology of Education) in the Department of Education and Professional Studies at King's College London as well as Honorary and Visiting Professor at the University of Hong Kong and Visiting Fellow at Beijing Normal University. Peter co-directed the SPRinG project and maintained responsibility for the Key Stage 1 developments. He has a long history of research and has published widely in this area. In addition to working with colleagues on the development of social pedagogy and the use of pupil groups, he was responsible for the development of the 'relational approach' that underlies effective grouping and interaction among children as well as co-developing theories and principles that underlie effective group working in preschools, primary and secondary schools.

Collaborating researchers

Anne Chowne is a teacher trainer who helped develop the Key Stage 2 ideas and activities with teachers and supported the implementation and evaluation of the SPRinG approach with Key Stage 2 teachers.

Cathy Ota and **Lucia Berdondini** were responsible for the co-development of Key Stage 1 activities and the initial structuring of material for the handbook. In particular, they worked with teachers to refine and implement the 'relational approach' and support systems for Key Stage 1 teachers, and they are responsible for the training organisation Working with Others.

Chapter 1

Background and introduction to the handbook

This handbook is the result of a four-year study that brought together teachers and researchers in the exploration of how pupil group work can be made more effective in support of children's learning. The research study, known as the 'SPRinG' project, developed and evaluated a new approach to group work in primary schools. It was funded by the Economic and Social Research Council's Teaching and Learning Research Programme. SPRinG is an acronym for Social Pedagogic Research into Group work, and is based upon the view that effective group work can be facilitated through:

1   careful attention to the physical and social organisation of the classroom and groups;
2   the development of pupils' group-working skills (based upon an inclusive relational approach, working with *all* children in a class);
3   the creation and structuring of challenging tasks that legitimise group work; and
4   the supportive involvement of teachers and other adults.

The project had two aims: first, to work with teachers to develop strategies which would enhance the quality of group and paired work; and, second, to evaluate whether these strategies would result in an improvement in pupils' attainment and learning, behaviour and attitudes to school. The original project evaluation involved 162 classes in primary and secondary schools, and 4,259 pupils aged 5 to 14. Based on the success of SPRinG, our approach has been taken-up in a number of different contexts, internationally and in urban and rural areas. This handbook focuses on children in primary schools but many features have also been found to work well in secondary schools or with even older students.

Findings from the research showed that engaging in the SPRinG group-work programme had a positive effect on all pupils. Group work led to gains in attainment and learning, greater levels of active classroom engagement and sustained discussions, and the clear sense among pupils and teachers that working in groups was a positive classroom experience.

What makes SPRinG distinctive?

The SPRinG approach applies group work across the curriculum and over the school year. We worked with teachers to develop a programme that could be successfully integrated into school life and the curriculum, and that recognised the concerns and difficulties teachers can have with group work. We were particularly concerned that the approach should not just dwell on a theory or dictate actions to the teacher – rather the SPRinG approach is a co-development between teachers and researchers. This collaboration enabled an approach informed by theory and hard evidence, which was field tested in many schools, and which is appropriate for use by children of different ages and in different cultures. The original collaboration between researchers and teachers extended for two years or more. Each class was expected to undertake at least two one-hour SPRinG group-work sessions per week.

One strength of the SPRinG programme is that it is based on a long-term systematic evaluation of pupil progress over a full school year and comparison with a control group in terms of objective measures of attainment and classroom behaviour.

What did we find?

Key finding 1

Far from impeding learning, group work raised levels of achievement. In the early years of primary school, group work helped to improve attainment in reading and mathematics. SPRinG activities for older primary school pupils were targeted at science and led to significantly higher attainment and deeper conceptual understanding and inferential thinking.

Key finding 2

Despite some teachers' worries that group work might be disruptive, pupil behaviour *improved* in the SPRinG classes. Children were able to take more responsibility for their own behaviour and learning, freeing up teacher time to observe and reflect upon classroom activities.

Key finding 3

Group work doubled pupils' levels of sustained, active engagement in learning and more than doubled the amount of high-level, thoughtful discussion between children.

Other findings

- Teachers' professional skills and confidence were enhanced and their teaching repertoire was extended. There were also unexpected benefits – for example, as pupils developed group-working skills, teachers found they were 'freed' from classroom control and were able to spend more time teaching.

- Group work seemed to be most effective when adopted by the whole school, rather than individual teachers.
- Teachers working in areas of deprivation or in difficult circumstances found that group work can be used successfully and aid classroom relationships and social inclusion.

The SPRinG programme

The practices and recommended activities in the handbook are based upon the collective wisdom of collaborating teachers and researchers, previous research, and the results of the SPRinG studies. The SPRinG programme is based on four key principles for successful group work:

- The classroom and pupil groups need to be strategically organised and managed. Attention to classroom-seating arrangements and the characteristics of groups – such as their size, composition and stability – over time can make group work more effective.
- Group-work skills have to be developed. We cannot just put children into groups and expect them to work well together. Based on a 'relational approach' that encourages children to want to work together, activities in the handbook are designed to help pupils trust and respect each other; communicate effectively through listening, explaining and sharing ideas; and plan, organise and evaluate their group work.
- Group-work activities should encourage group work. Careful attention to the nature and structure of activities can ensure that group work is productive and supports the further development of group-working skills.
- Adults should adopt a range of roles that are supportive of group work and that encourage pupil independence rather than teaching pupils directly or dominating group interactions.

Each of these four principles is the subject of a chapter in this book (see Chapters 4 to 7 respectively).

Getting children to work together is not easy and requires perseverance, reflection, problem-solving and a host of other skills on the part of both the teacher and pupils. The positive aspects of effective group work take time and planning. They certainly are not learned over night, and it may take some time before you notice a clear change in the capabilities of your pupils. However, the rewards reported by many teachers and our findings concerning pupil development are worthy of the effort that is invested. Group work offers learning possibilities for pupils not provided by either teacher-led or individual work, and can help to improve attitudes to work and classroom behaviour. We hope that this handbook will lead to more systematic use of group work in classrooms and across the curriculum and the school. It deserves to be given a more central role in educational policy and school practice.

Since the first SPRinG study, we have undertaken similar studies in other parts of the world. Even within a developed country such as the UK, there are distinct differences between urban and rural schools. In rural schools, especially primary schools, pupils tend to know each other better and engage in collective activity, and it may be assumed that there would be greater group work effects in urban schools. The extension of SPRinG in Scotland (ScotSPRinG) showed that children in both urban and rural schools benefitted academically and socially – even though the rural children had a social 'head start'.

Extensions of SPRinG have also seen success in preschool/early years education across northern and southern Europe. Studies were undertaken in Finland, Sweden, Greece, Italy, Spain and the United Kingdom. Working with teacher/practitioners of 4-year-olds over time showed increased levels of interaction among children, a greater ability for children to work autonomously from the teacher and higher levels of cognitive understanding. SPRinG extension studies also took place in primary schools in Confucian Heritage Cultures (CHC) in Hong Kong and Shanghai. In Hong Kong classrooms there has traditionally been an approach that involves a lot of teacher direction and where pupils do not engage in discussion and are often placed in competition with one another. Yet, the introduction of a SPRinG approach to primary school mathematics classrooms in Hong Kong showed that pupils could easily adapt to group working, that their achievement levels improved considerably and improved achievement was associated with increased dialogue (e.g. questions, answers, explanations) between classroom peers. The CHC actually encouraged teacher commitment and legitimisation of the new approach and less obviously encouraged pupil informal commitment to help one another outside of the classroom.

SPRinG extensions have also taken place in Caribbean countries. Similar to CHC, the school systems here are noted for their traditional, teacher-dominated and competitive approaches to pupil learning. Yet with SPRinG, pupils showed increased academic and social development. Of particular interest was that all students improved academically – with the greatest improvement among those pupils initially identified as 'low attainers'. Teachers, too, realised that low attaining pupils had much to contribute to their classes.

Each of these applications of SPRinG shows that the ideas and approaches developed in SPRinG can contribute to children's educational and social development, and that this handbook can be used successfully in many different countries around the world.

Why should I want to use this book?

It is not easy to develop effective group-work skills among pupils. This handbook offers recommendations for practice to help you make group work effective for you and your class. There are also ideas to help you resolve particular problems associated with group work that can arise in a class or group and suggested training activities to support pupils in developing a positive group ethos and particular group skills.

Although the main audience for this book is likely to be staff who work with primary school-aged children, many of the ideas, principles and practices also apply to the use of group work in secondary and further education contexts. Readers wishing to undertake group work with adolescents and young adults may wish to use and adjust the practices in the suggested ways, for example, by increasing the group size slightly to make the group work more challenging or by getting the young people to plan their group roles and the activity themselves.

Similarly, group work may appear to 'fit' more readily with the educational traditions and practices of schools in Westernised cultural contexts. However, as we have seen, our research has shown that schools in other cultural contexts can make good use of peer co-learning. If teachers and their students are committed to the development of group-working skills, there is often a collective or collaborative basis within all societies to support effective group working. However, teachers in all cultures may need to work hard to legitimise pupil efforts in group work.

The ideas in this handbook aim to support the development of effective group working. They can be used in conjunction with ideas from other educational initiatives that focus on debate and discussion, problem-solving, critical-thinking and general-thinking skills initiatives. Good examples of these are: 'Philosophy for Children', 'Thinking Together', 'Thinking Maps', 'Habits of Mind', 'Six Hat Thinking' and 'Building Learning Power' – all useful programmes for developing thinking and dialogue; there are, of course, many others that are useful as well. Group-work practices should help enhance the overall effectiveness of these initiatives.

Why this second edition?

We were pleased to be asked to write a second edition of this handbook. While retaining what is felt are the key features of the programme and the suggested activities, we have expanded the text in several ways. Given what we see as the important role of the whole school and school leadership in the sustained success of group work, we have added a completely new chapter (Chapter 10) in which we describe a number of steps that can be taken to ensure that group work is embedded in a whole school approach and procedures. We have also extended the text in several chapters, for example, in relation to the growing international use of collaborative approaches. Since the first edition the authors have visited and undertaken research in countries around the world and have become even more aware of the potential for group work. All the authors have also supervised many masters and doctoral level students from around the world, and learned valuable lessons from the research undertaken on group work in these countries. We have also further developed and consolidated our theoretical approach to group work on the basis of many journal papers and book chapters and a book length treatment of the whole primary level SPRinG project. Since the first edition in the UK there has been a rapid growth in extra adults in classrooms – especially Teaching Assistants (TAs) – which has had implications for the role of adults leading group work. This handbook deals with this new development and draws on the largest study worldwide on the deployment and impact of TAs (The DISS project). Finally, we have extended the text with additional quotes from the many teachers that were involved in the research and case studies from schools, and draw on valuable feedback from users of the first edition.

Structure of this handbook

The handbook is composed of two parts: the first provides recommendations and information about how group work can be successfully used and implemented in primary school classrooms; the second provides examples of a developmental programme of activities.

In Chapter 2 we outline the case for group work, providing an explanation as to why it can be a powerful learning context and information on how best to use this book. Chapter 3 encourages teachers to reflect on how their classrooms are currently organised and the success of group work in their classes. Chapters 4 to 7 provide details of each of the key principles and the recommended practices for improving the effectiveness of group work and pupils' group-work skills. Chapter 8 provides suggestions and tools to help teachers and pupils reflect on and evaluate group work. Working from simple forms of group work to more complex group projects, Chapter 9 provides suggestions on how to start utilising group work in the curriculum. The new Chapter 10 outlines how best to implement group work across a whole school and provides suggestions on how to monitor and evaluate its effects on pupils and staff. Chapter 11 offers a range of useful ideas for overcoming common difficulties with group work.

The units in Part II provide a selection of group-work training activities designed to develop pupils' social, communication and advanced group-work skills. These activities are organised into a developmental sequence that aims to build up group-working skills incrementally. These activities can be supplemented with your own ideas.

How to use this handbook

You are most likely reading this book as teacher, headteacher or as someone who assists the teacher and pupils within a class who is interested in group work. In our experience, the ideas presented here are best used as part of a whole school approach to developing group-work skills (see Chapter 10). As a teacher or teaching assistant on your own, we feel that you will also find the content of this guide very useful, though we suggest that you may increase the likelihood of success if you work through the ideas and training activities with other teachers and colleagues.

There are a number of ways to utilise the ideas and activities presented here. We recommend that before the school year starts you read, think about and set up your classroom in preparation for group work (Chapters 3 and 4); then implement the group-training (sequential) activities to build up trust, sensitivity and respect within the class (see Chapter 5). Use some of the early activities in Part II to get an idea of which children may work well with each other (though this should not be the only reason for putting them together) before creating your groups. Try to use circle time, social/emotional education or personal/health education sessions to support this process and initiate the sharing of feelings and perspectives and the build-up of trust. Think about how you can arrange resources and tasks in your classroom to enhance group working (Chapter 6) and how you and other adults in the classroom can support group work without being too directive (Chapter 7).

At the same time, it is worthwhile to begin to use some simple forms of group work in addition to the training activities (e.g., pairs or talk partners) in your lessons (Chapter 9). For example, instead of directing questions to individuals in class, ask children to find partners and have them decide on joint responses to your questions. Ask children (maybe of different ages/abilities) to share a book and take turns reading paragraphs to each other. With further training you can begin to scale up the use of partner work to full group work and to increase the amount of group work you do with pupils across the curriculum.

We recommend that two sessions of group work activities per week is the bare minimum for children to start making progress and for developing group-work skills. There may be points where you would want to increase or reduce the intensity of group work. For example, during the 'storming' stage, when arguments are frequent and group work can be stressful (see Chapter 4), increasing the amount of group work will help children advance and resolve the problems. By the end of training it is important that classes regularly practice, reinforce and reflect on their group-work skills. Debriefing (see Chapter 5), or reflecting on the success (and failure) of group working, is an essential group-working skill and, again, this may be particularly important when children are experiencing difficulties.

You will find that you have curriculum constraints and time pressures that may prevent you from using group work as much as you would like. One successful approach is to set aside a slot for group work (as above, we suggest at least twice a week). If you persist, you will also find that there are many places in the curriculum where group and paired work can be undertaken (e.g. during personal/health and social/emotional education, literacy, numeracy, physical education, science and so on). And, as your class becomes more competent in group working, it will become easier to integrate it as part of the curriculum.

The training activities (in Part II) are as much for your benefit as for that of your pupils. These activities provide illustrations of the application of the main practices recommended in the first part of the handbook. We are sure you can improve on them both as effective activities and in terms of the fun that children have while doing them. Please be creative, and try to be supportive of colleagues who are developing and using these activities. These activities are just a snapshot of the range of possible fun training activities available, and we encourage you to look widely for other activities. It is important however to make sure that new activities that you try really do warrant working together and encourage the social and communicative and decision-making skills required for working as part of a group.

Further information

Further details of the findings of the original SPRinG study and subsequent studies can be found at www.spring-project.org.uk and in the book that brings together the findings from the main English and Scottish SPRinG studies:

Kutnick, P. & Blatchford, P. with Baines, E. & Tolmie, A. (2014). *Effective Group Work in Primary Schools*. London: Springer.

More detailed information is provided in the following published articles and reports:

Baines, E., Blatchford, P. & Chowne, A. (2007). 'Improving the effectiveness of collaborative group work in primary schools: Effects on science attainment'. ESRC Teaching and Learning Research Programme special issue of the *British Educational Research Journal*, *33*, 663–80.

Baines, E., Blatchford, P. & Kutnick, P. (2008). 'Pupil grouping for learning: Developing a social pedagogy of the classroom', in R. Gillies, A. Ashman & J. Terwel (eds.), *The Teacher's Role in Implementing Cooperative Learning in the Classroom*. New York: Springer-Verlag.

Baines, E., Blatchford, P. & Webster, R. (2015). 'The challenges of implementing group-work in primary school classrooms and including pupils with Special Educational Needs'. Special issue of *Education 3-13, 43*, 15–29.

Baines, E., Rubie-Davies, C. & Blatchford, P. (2009). 'Improving pupil group work interaction and dialogue in primary classrooms: Results from a year-long intervention study'. *Cambridge Journal of Education, 39*, 95–117.

Blatchford, P., Baines, E., Kutnick, P. & Galton, M. (2005). 'Improving pupil group work in classrooms: A new approach to increasing engagement and learning in everyday classroom settings at Key Stages 1, 2 and 3'. *ESRC TLRP Research Briefing 11, Nov 2005*. Retrieved from www.tlrp.org

Blatchford, P., Baines, E., Rubie-Davies, C., Bassett, P. & Chowne, A. (2006). 'The effect of a new approach to group work on pupil–pupil and teacher–pupil interactions'. *Journal of Educational Psychology, 98*, 750–65.

Blatchford, P., Galton, M., Kutnick, P. & Baines, E. (2005). 'Improving the effectiveness of pupil groups in classrooms'. Final Report to ESRC (Ref: L139 25 1046).

Blatchford, P., Kutnick, P., Baines, E. & Galton, M. (2003). 'Toward a social pedagogy of classroom group work'. *International Journal of Educational Research, 39*, 153–72.

Galton, M. & Hargreaves, L. (2009). 'Group work: still a neglected art?' *Cambridge Journal of Education, 39*, 1–6.

Galton, M., Hargreaves, L. & Pell, T. (2009). 'Group work and whole class teaching with 11- to 14-year-olds compared'. *Cambridge Journal of Education, 39*(1), 119–40.

Galton, M., Steward, S., Hargreaves, L., Page, C. & Pell, A. (2009). *Motivating your secondary class*. London: SAGE.

Kutnick, P. (2015). 'Developing effective group work in classrooms: A relational approach within a culturally appropriate pedagogy'. In R. M. Gillies (ed.), *Cooperative Learning: Developments in Research and Practice*. New York: Nova Science.

Kutnick, P. & Berdondini, L. (2009). 'Can the enhancement of group working in classrooms provide a basis for effective communication in support of school-based cognitive achievement in classrooms of young learners'. *Cambridge Journal of Education, 39*, 71–94.

Kutnick, P., Fung, D. Mok, I. & Leung, F. with Lee, B.P-Y, & Mai, Y. Y. (in press). 'Implementing effective group work for mathematical understanding in primary school classrooms in Hong Kong'. *International Journal of Science and Mathematics Education*.

Kutnick, P., Genta, M. L., Brighi, A. & Sasavini, A. (2008). *Relational Approaches in Early Education: Enhancing Social Inclusion and Personal Growth for Learning*. Bologna: Cooperativa Libraria Universitaria Editrice Bologna.

Kutnick, P., Layne, A., Jules, V. & Layne, C. (2008). 'Academic achievement, participation and groupwork skills in secondary school classrooms in the Caribbean'. *International Journal of Educational Development, 28*, 176–94.

Kutnick, P., Ota, C. & Berdondini, L. (2008). 'Improving the effects of group working in classrooms with young school-aged children: Facilitating attainment, interaction and classroom activity'. *Learning and Instruction*, *18*, 83–95.

Pell, T., Galton, M., Steward, S., Page, C. & Hargreaves, L. (2007). 'Promoting group work at Key stage 3: Solving an attitudinal crisis among adolescents'. *Research Papers in Education*, *22*, 309–32.

Part I

Developing group work in your classroom

Chapter 2

The case for group work

One of the most important aspects of growing up is learning how to interact and work with others. The skills involved are used in our everyday social interactions with others, at work and at home. But the skills that underpin group work (what we refer to as 'group-working skills') are often taken for granted and assumed to develop fairly naturally through our everyday interactions with family, friends and acquaintances.

The school context is perhaps the first opportunity where children from diverse backgrounds come together and have the opportunity to interact. In school, children are often told how they should and should not behave and work. But they are rarely given the opportunity to learn how to interact and work with others or to reflect on these interactions and their interpersonal skills. Some of the skills involved can be socially and/or intellectually complex: for example, sustaining a discussion on a topic, explaining reasoning, helping others without over-helping, developing an argument or counter-argument, reaching a consensus or compromise, bringing others into the discussion, planning group work and so on. It is important that teachers and schools provide opportunities for children to learn these essential social skills so that they can gain more from future learning opportunities and take a more active role in their own learning in the future.

We also know that in any classroom there are three main learning contexts. First, there are those involving interactions between the teacher and pupils in the class. Second, there are those when children are working on their own on a task. The third is when children are working with each other. We know from much research in primary and secondary schools over many years that children spend much of their time either listening to the teacher or working on their own, but it is unlikely that you will see children working together on a task. They can be seated in groups, of course, but they are not often working together *as* a group. On the other hand, children spend much more classroom time in the presence of their peers than with a teacher or working on their own.

When groups are organised in classrooms, it is often in the interest of classroom management, ability differentiation and in response to the classroom layout. There is little sign of a pedagogic relationship between features of groupings, such as group size, learning purposes or the nature of the task set. Research has also shown that teachers have little faith in pupils' ability to work in groups, and pupils rarely have the skills to prepare themselves for group work. There is a vicious cycle at work in that teachers' beliefs are consistent with the difficulties they encounter with group work, while pupils' behaviour in groups and lack of success in turn confirm some teachers' belief that group work is of little value.

It is our view that effective group work does not receive the recognition it deserves and hardly figures into educational policies for primary schools. But when used well, group work can enhance pupils' learning, motivation and ability to work together, and can encourage children to be less dependent on the teacher by taking more responsibility for their own behaviour and learning. Teachers also benefit as we show below.

The case for group work is becoming stronger each year. As the availability of information is ever more present and the means of accessing that information ever more immediate, the importance of helping students make sense of that information through discussion becomes more marked. Education is as much about making sense of information as imparting it. Employers often complain that students leaving school and even university may have academic achievements to their name but do not have the problem-solving skills or the communication skills needed for modern forms of employment. In the twenty-first century the case for learning the skills for working together is very strong. Interestingly, this is now widely recognised in East Asian countries and regions like Shanghai, Hong Kong, Taiwan, Macao and Japan. It is often assumed that these high performing countries and regions, on international comparisons like the PISA tests, rely on traditional teacher led methods of instruction. However, in recent years there have been strong government led drives in many of these places toward a more learner-centred and collaborative approach to education in primary schools.

What is group work?

There is more to group work than sitting pupils in groups and asking them to work together. By 'group work' we mean just that – pupils working together as a group or team for a joint purpose or outcome. The children may work on a practical task, on a problem that requires one solution, brainstorming or discussing views on a local issue about which views are strong. We argue that group work can be used across all curriculum areas, and for many different types of task. In this handbook our emphasis is on developing group-work skills that support learning, and, in particular, activities that encourage high level talk and discussion as well as high level thinking skills (e.g. analysing, evaluating and synthesising). Teachers are central in setting up and supporting effective group work and its development, but the particular feature of group work – perhaps its defining characteristic – is that *the balance of ownership and control of the work shifts towards the pupils themselves*.

There are many subtly different approaches to group work, and it is often referred to in different ways. Some call it 'cooperative learning' or 'cooperative group work', others call it 'collaborative group work' and some talk about 'peer tutoring' or 'peer-assisted learning'. These are all different in rather subtle ways. Cooperative group work emphasises children's interdependent skills being used towards a common goal, and collaborative group work emphasises the use of dialogue to reach understanding. But our notion of effective group work is more inclusive than any one single approach. Effective group work involves two or more persons working together to undertake a learning task as *co-learners*, and it incorporates all types of peer learning – from cooperative and collaborative group work to peer tutoring and peer helping or assistance. Its inclusive nature is likely to encourage higher levels of participation and engagement for every child in the class. We particularly stress the prior importance of helping children develop the relational skills to relate well with one another and seeing the benefits of working with all members of their class. This is vital if group work is to be effective.

For group work to be successful children need to take joint responsibility for undertaking and contributing to the group activity. In contrast to some other approaches to peer learning, we do not advocate the view that individual accountability (to the teacher and/or class) is crucial for peer learning to be successful. We suggest that public and forced efforts to make participants accountable (e.g. through awarding prizes, individual scores or by structuring the task so that participants feel obliged to participate) are unnecessary and can even undermine children's feelings of safety and trust of other group members. This in turn can reduce the enjoyment, informality and feelings of relative safety that arise in the context of group work, and may discourage certain class members from wanting to participate. Group members do, however, need to be accountable to each other, and this is why an approach that focuses on enhancing positive social relations between pupils is important. Encouraging children to adopt particular social skills and positive social attitudes, trust, mutual respect, and sensitivity toward other group members and class mates, and offering opportunities for reflection on how the group is working, all help encourage children to want to participate and be jointly accountable to each other for group work. Similarly, offering fun, carefully structured activities, in well-planned groups also helps.

What are the benefits of effective group work?

There is now an extensive literature on the benefits of group work in schools. In brief, it has been found to help in the following areas (see Further information, p. 94):

- Learning and conceptual development
- School achievement
- Engagement in learning and time on task
- Oracy development
- Critical, creative and analytical thinking skills
- Motivation and attitudes
- Confidence to express and explain opinions and thoughts with peers
- Behaviour in class and relationships between peers

It seems clear that we cannot teach children to behave in socially responsible and inclusive ways – this is not something that can be learned by instruction alone, like reading or subtraction. Behaving in a constructive way in relation to others is best furthered by children being given opportunities to work with others, to discuss and recognise alternative points of view, and by being held responsible for their own behaviour in a supportive atmosphere. Children learn to get on with each other not by being taught but through everyday encounters with peers. Quite apart from these academic benefits, group work can be great fun and very rewarding. Teachers also benefit from pupil group work. When children work together in a supportive and autonomous manner, teachers are less pressed by procedural and behavioural issues in the classroom, allowing greater attention to the process of enhancing children's learning.

A teacher's view – the benefits of group work

Generally it [training and group work] makes them more aware of being cooperative and helps their behaviour in and outside the classroom, their attitude and motivation to learn, the more confident you feel the more you learn. I think it helps children's confidence a lot.

(Facilitator, School 5, P5)*

Why does it work?

There are several theories that explain why group work is beneficial for learning. One view is that children's conceptual development can be facilitated by coming up against the differing views of others at about the same level of development. The 'cognitive conflict' this causes can force children to adjust and develop their own way of seeing and explaining things, and hence promote learning and conceptual development. A second view is that the process of explaining something and listening to the explanations of others involves a greater depth of thinking and a more integrated understanding of ideas. This explains, in particular, why peer tutoring/helping can enhance the learning of both the tutor and the pupil being tutored. There is nothing like having to teach something to someone else to really get to know it oneself. A third view is that when children work together they can arrive at solutions to problems and understanding of concepts that would not have been possible if they had worked alone. We all have different ideas and thoughts on how best to do things, and children can feed off and explore each other's ideas; they can learn together and make use of this knowledge and understanding when on their own. But in order for children to benefit from working with others, they have to want to work together as a group; they must feel safe and secure with one another; and they must feel prepared and supported in their group-working skills.

* Note: this source information identifies whether the interviewee was a group work 'Facilitator' (usually a senior teacher trained in the group working methods used) or a 'Teacher' or part of a group discussion of teachers (teachers were supported and trained by the facilitator). The school where the respondent came from is identified along with the page number of the transcript from which the quote was drawn. More information on these data and the approach to the research can be found in: Kutnick, P. & Blatchford, P. with Baines, E. & Tolmie, A. (2014). *Effective Group Work in Primary Schools*. London: Springer.

Children need to feel secure in the knowledge that the peers in the group (and the class) will not laugh at them, humiliate or tease them in front of others or otherwise respond negatively if they make a mistake or express particular ideas or views. Without such feelings of safety and security, working in a group may result in a negative experience. This may be particularly important in the case of groups of children who might not usually mix - for example, children from different ethnic or ability groups, or girls and boys.

Why do I need to use group work with my class?

This is an important question. Of course there are many different approaches to teaching and learning and many of the current and widely used approaches are good at helping young people learn. A fundamental aspect of the approach underpinning this handbook is that teaching and learning practices need to be used strategically for different learning purposes. We have called this a 'social pedagogic' approach to highlight the way that learning takes place in a social context and that teaching, grouping arrangements, the task and curriculum need to be strategically aligned for effective learning. Certain types of learning come from certain types of teaching. For instance, there are times when it can be best to work and learn on our own, for example, when practicing a recently learned skill or deciding what our own view is about something - sometimes this can be informed by others' views, but nevertheless there is a need within the learning process for independent learning. Similarly there are times when whole class teaching and discussion will facilitate the wider sharing of views or new ideas. But there are also times when children working together as part of group will enable more efficient and more effective learning. As a result of group work, the knowledge that group members gain is likely to have been thought through more rigorously, shared and adapted in the light of what others have said. There are also a range of additional benefits that can come from the use of peer co-learning and group work that do not necessarily follow from more traditional approaches to teaching and learning. Group work can be very exciting, fun, rewarding, creative and inherently motivating. Many students have described group work as more informal, more natural and sometimes not like schoolwork at all, but more fun. As a result, children become more autonomous as learners. They are more likely to ask each other for help rather than being dependent on adults in the class. So this makes for a less demanding and dependent class of pupils, and can improve your professional development as well.

A teacher's view – the ideas in this book can support professional development

I feel like my teaching has altered. I'm more adventurous myself and I suppose more child centred ... for them to discover and work together, less controlling, basically.

(Teacher 2, School 4, P3)

Group-work training and repeated experiences of peer co-learning can enhance children's social skills and the relationships amongst children in the class, and provide them with conflict resolution strategies that are helpful for resolving minor fallings out. So there is a place for effective group work in every classroom, and it may enhance the impact of learning when combined with other approaches to learning.

But I already do group work

It is a common view amongst teachers that they already undertake quite a lot of group work in their classrooms. This may be the case of course, though we have found that teachers can overestimate the extent and quality of the group work taking place, and close observation may show it to be actually quite limited, for example, to paired discussions prompted by the teacher. In many classrooms, the group table is the prominent seating arrangement for children, but this does not mean that children engage in effective group work.

It is useful to try to be certain about whether children are working together *as a* group or team or whether they are just working *in* a group. Even if children appear to be talking and working together, it may be useful to monitor whether this talk is completely focused on the activity, tangential, low level or even off topic. It might be useful to review Chapter 3, How is your classroom organised?, to see whether you are really getting the best out of any group that you have set up; there are likely to be ways to make the group work more productive.

But even if you do group work, this book can help in a different way – by facilitating new ideas about extending or developing the group work that you do or by helping you make it even more effective. This book may provide food for thought that can inspire you in other ways so that you become more sure of your own ideas and thinking.

The children in my class are not ready to undertake group work

Some teachers feel that their children are too young, do not have the skills to work together or cannot be trusted to work together without getting into arguments and fights. Children, especially young ones, are in many respects still learning the skills that will enable them to function effectively as a member of a group. It is important to remember that this is not a straightforward process, and that even many adults have reservations and difficulties working with others. Developing the skills to work effectively and efficiently with others can take many years to develop, and even then each group situation can be different. However, we have found that teachers can create a cycle of expectation within which children, because they are not expected to work well together, are not given the opportunity or training to do so, and they then do not work well together. This thus confirms the initial negative view! If children never get the chance to work with others, or are never encouraged to think about how they can avoid or resolve squabbles and arguments, then they may never fully learn these skills.

To take on group work in this way requires a leap of faith – but it's definitely worth it!

Advice from teachers.

Can the ideas in this handbook be used with older children and young people or in schools in other cultural contexts?

There is no reason why the principles and recommended practices in this book cannot be used to help organise and plan for group work with students at any level. The ideas presented in Chapters 3 through 11 apply in principle just as much to secondary and further education contexts as they do in primary education. Part II of this handbook is largely designed to train primary school-aged children in social, communicational and other group-working skills, though, even in this part of the book, there may be ideas that can be used for supporting older children in the group work (e.g. the unit on group work and group-work rules).

One key to effective group work in different countries or with different-aged children is the role of the teacher. No matter which country, teachers must be committed to group work – legitimising its use in the classroom. Teachers will need to listen to group problems and ask the class how these can be resolved. With support from the teacher and developing of group-work skills among children in classrooms, effective group work can be found in almost any context. We have good evidence that children as young as 4 years can engage and gain from effective group work – developing inclusive groups, sharing ideas and working more autonomously from their teachers. Even with cultures in which teachers have been attributed traditional roles of knowledge and control, the implementation of group work has encouraged children to become more engaged in classroom learning and move away from learning passivity. There may be different constraints in different institutional and/or local cultural contexts that will require minor adaptation of the ideas in this handbook, but there is no reason why group work cannot be used in all classrooms, at all levels and in all locations around the world.

Chapter 3

How is your classroom organised?

In order to make best use of the principles, practices and group-training activities in the sections that follow, it is important to think about the layout and the grouping practices you employ in your classroom.

How is your classroom grouped for learning?

Your classroom is a very complicated 'site' for learning and interaction. One way of developing an understanding of your classroom and the way in which you use pupil groups is to 'map' pupils and their learning activity during a lesson. Classroom mapping provides a lot of information about pupil groups and their relationship to learning. Have a look at the following examples (see Figures 3.1, 3.2 and 3.3).

In the first map, drawn from a classroom in England, we see a relatively small class size (by UK standards) and we see there are individual pupils working, a number of pairs of pupils, a small group of six pupils working with a teacher (A), and a number of subject-based tasks. Note that most of the children are working either in pairs or in a small group; some of these groups mix boys (M) and girls (F), but others are single sex. The teacher is working with only one group of pupils (Group 7). There is another adult, a teaching assistant (TA), who is working with a boy with special educational needs (SEN) outside the classroom (Group 9).

We suggest that you draw a map of your own classroom. Though not essential, it may be more fruitful if you do this when pupils are working together on an activity. To make a map:

1   Begin by drawing a plan of your classroom before the lesson. Include work areas, desks and other main features.
2   When a lesson is in full swing and everyone is working, bring out your plan and pencil in where everyone is seated/working (noting, where possible, boys and girls, and each child's level of attainment for that subject). Include yourself, teaching assistants and other adults in the plan. Put a circle around those children and adults who are supposed to be working together as a group on a single activity. Take a few moments to assess what is going on within each grouping or at each table.
3   During break time/recess, or soon after the lesson, note down: (a) the nature of the task in which each grouping (individual, class or group) was engaged; (b)

the nature of the interaction between pupils (working jointly on the learning task, working in parallel on the same task and informally allowed to talk or help each other, or working independently on different tasks); and (c) any other thoughts and comments relating to the extent to which children were working together, working alone, actively engaged in thoughtful conversation about the work, the extent to which they were on or passively off task or drawing other pupils off task.

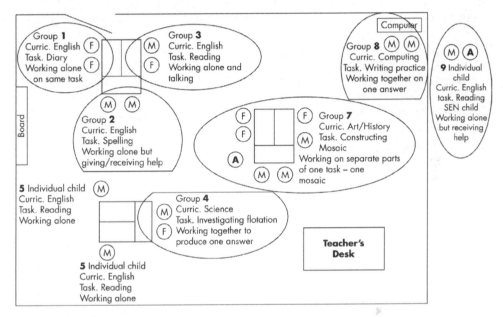

Figure 3.1 A classroom map

We have found that many teachers and researchers have used this simple technique to draw out valuable information; it is a very useful way to help you reflect on the range of practices and the nature and amount of group work that you do.

When you have more time, use the mapping as a memory aid to reflect on the lesson. The following questions will help you:

- How much was the classroom activity adult led?
- How often and for how long did students get to speak?
- What proportion of the class regularly contributes to class discussions?
- Would students find value in discussing their work, views and understanding with peers?
- How much independent work was going on?
- During independent work, how much talk with peers was there and to what extent was this task-based or social/off task?
- To what extent did students working alone disrupt other students?
- How much group work was going on? Is there potential for more group work to be undertaken in your lessons?

- How was the TA deployed in the classroom – did he or she work exclusively with a group comprising low attaining pupils and those with SEN? How far did the TA support or lead the child's or group's work?

You should use your answers relative to these questions to think about your arrangements and practices more generally to help you evaluate how much peer co-learning goes on in your class, the nature of the activities that take place and how pupils are supported in their learning. It is also useful to begin to think about the occasions when peer co-learning can be easily introduced and easily supported.

Here is another example map (see Figure 3.2) of a different classroom layout. In this map, the classroom is arranged in a double horseshoe shape, and the teacher is teaching the whole class from the front. There are no additional adults present. In this instance, there is only one grouping since the class is all working together to focus on a single activity. This is an ideal seating arrangement for whole class interactive teaching and for pupils potentially to work independently or in pairs. The arrangement is also useful for a teacher to move around the class monitoring pupils' work, asking them questions and to work with a particular group for a sustained period, using the central horseshoe to bring different small groups of children together. It may be less easy to see how this classroom layout would work for small groups of three and four, and it is likely that this arrangement may

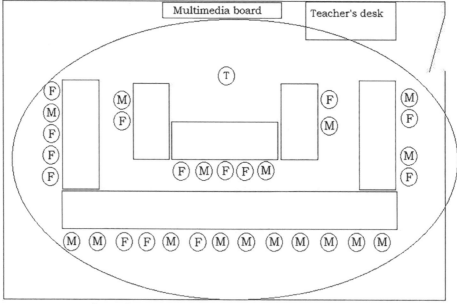

Group 1
Curriculum: English
Task: Story comprehension
Whole class teaching - pupils listen to teacher speak and answer questions

Figure 3.2 A classroom map – horseshoe arrangement

unwittingly 'lead' the teacher to use whole class discourse and individual working as the dominant approaches to learning. But there are straightforward possibilities to bring in more peer co-learning and group work into the classroom. For example, pupils in the inner horseshoe can turn around to create small groups with those behind them. Other students might locate themselves at the ends of tables or on the other side, again to enable face-to-face interactions and small group working (see Figure 3.3). There may need to be some movement of tables to move groups away from each other so that group members do not have to compete with the noise coming from other groups to make themselves heard.

It is also useful to map out or reflect on a recent time when you used group or paired work to help you think about how you might improve these occasions. The following questions relate primarily to peer co-learning situations.

The organisation of the classroom and groups

- How far were the layout of the classroom and seating arrangements conducive to comfortable group working? If not, can they be easily rearranged to make them more suitable for group working?
- Were pupils sufficiently close together so that they could work together quietly?
- Could pupils within the groups see each other sufficiently well to allow good communication?
- Did the size of groups allow all pupils to get thoroughly involved in the group interaction?

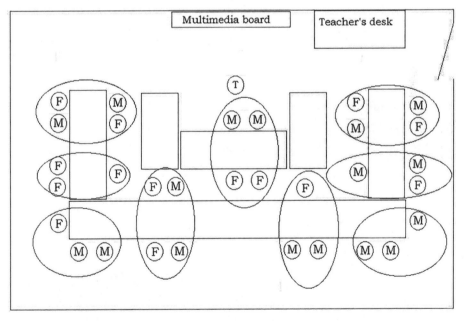

Figure 3.3 A classroom map – horseshoe arrangement set up for group working

- Were all members of the groups involved in the work and interaction or did pupils from one gender group or ability level tend to opt out?

For more information on preparing your classroom for group work, see Chapter 4.

Pupils' skills and group interactions

- Did the groups work effectively?
- Was the conversation primarily focused on the work that was being undertaken?
- Were there squabbles between group members? Were children able to compromise or resolve conflicts?
- Did some pupils dominate the interaction and work?
- Did shy pupils feel sufficiently comfortable to contribute to group interactions?

For more information on developing pupil's group working skills, see Chapter 5.

Group-work task

- Did the activity encourage pupils to discuss the content of the task or were conversations mostly about resources?
- Did children in the group end up working on their own and producing their own piece of work or was there a single group outcome?
- Did the group manage to plan and undertake all aspects of the task or did they lose their way?
- Were group members able to manage given roles and sustain a responsibility to undertake the group activity?

For more information on creating effective tasks for group work, see Chapter 6.

Adult role in relation to group work

- Were the children able to work independently of adult support?
- Were the children constantly seeking direction and support from adults?
- Did you and the Teaching Assistant encourage pupils to think for themselves, to make their own decisions and manage their own time?
- How far was the group work and outcome independent of an adult's input?

For more information about how adults can support groups, see Chapter 7.

Think about ...

The following may help prepare you for taking on the recommended group-work practices and group-work training activities with your class. Think about:

- how you might be able to do things differently so that you can incorporate more group work;
- when you will prepare your classroom for group work;
- how you will implement group training sessions into your weekly lesson timetable; and
- how you can convince others, including your headteacher, to adopt a whole school approach to group work.

Chapter 4

Preparing the classroom for successful group work

Group work requires preparation of the classroom. Seating arrangements and group organisation can have a profound effect on peer support, communication and work in groups. To understand and use groups effectively in your classroom, pay particular attention to:

- class seating arrangements;
- group size;
- number of groups;
- group stability; and
- group composition.

Class seating arrangements

It is important that seating arrangements support group working. Flexible use of furniture and seating can make a big difference. *Using and coordinating the physical layout, seating arrangement and space to encourage pupil interaction in different working situations is key.*

- *Whole class interactive work* is best undertaken when children are seated in a dedicated space, sometimes on the floor on a mat or carpet. If the aim is to facilitate a class discussion, children are best seated in a circle, or better still, multiple layers of a small circle where they can see each other and the teacher (e.g. see Figure 3.2 in Chapter 3). To facilitate good group discussion, children need to be able to sit face to face and relatively near to each other. Alternatively, if the aim is for children to engage with the teacher, then having children sit facing the teacher in rows, pairs or in a horseshoe arrangement encourages engagement and concentration and makes it easier for the teacher to know that the students are paying attention. Avoid having children sitting with their backs to each other or to you.
- *Individual work* is most effective when done in individual seats, but if space is limited, in pairs, rows or other ways that discourage potential distraction, it is better that children do not sit opposite each other.
- *Paired work* works best when pupils are seated in pairs/rows or as small groups where working partners sit next to/across from each other.

- *Group work* is most likely to be successful when children are seated in small groups around a *single* standard rectangular table or around the corner of a larger table. If children are seated in a line or are not facing each other, try to move them so that they are face to face and relatively close together. When children sit closer together there is less noise and they are more likely to get involved. Only increase the space if the group needs to use materials and books. Encourage children to organise themselves so that they can see each other and are not stuck out on the edge.

If the furniture is moved in set ways, and regularly, pupils become accustomed to this and movement will take less time with practice. The *physical space* available may constrain your flexibility, but, even in the smallest of classrooms, there are ways to adjust how pupils sit and the direction they face.

Advice from teachers – flexible furniture arrangements

This class, they've become used to moving tables around very quickly. They're absolutely very quick at making sure there's four on a big table; however, if there's three, what I've found is that they try to climb the tables to look at the sheet etc. so they found that if they just go into the corner [of the table], one sits in the corner and the other two there, that's much better. In fact, these tables are a bit too big for four; they think so as well. Seeing each other is important.

(Facilitator, School 6, P2)

Group size

The size of groups that are to undertake group work should be appropriate to the age and experience of pupils and the purpose of the group task. Groups should normally consist of no more than four or five pupils by the end of the primary school, and the group size may be smaller when pupils are learning how to interact together and at the start of primary school. Pairs are more likely to guarantee pupil involvement than any other group size. As group size increases *free rider* behaviour (when a member lets others do all the work) becomes more probable, *communication* becomes increasingly difficult, and *diffusion of responsibility* (where no one feels responsible for doing the work) is more likely.

Pairs and threes should be used to introduce group working to pupils.

Pros	Cons
• Simpler for pupils to work in. • Helps build confidence for work in larger groups. • Good for encouraging young and shy pupils to interact. • Good when the task is complex, requiring different perspectives to enhance learning. • Good for peer tutoring. • Free riding and diffusion of responsibility unlikely. • Threes are good for practising decision making and consensus.	• One child can dominate. • Can be too easy if task is too simple, as in a practice task. • In threes, one child can be marginalised.

Small groups of four to six pupils are good for many group-work activities, particularly for collaborative tasks allowing members to cope with planning, discussing, decision making, reaching consensus, managing interruptions and conflict and staying on topic/task.

Pros	Cons
• Good for group discussion, problem solving, group investigations and projects. • Good for bringing together different views.	• Small groups (four to six) represent more risk (threats to personal self-esteem and confidence) than smaller groups. • Members may be less likely to speak. • Free rider behaviour and diffusion of responsibility are more likely.

Large groups of seven to ten pupils are difficult to manage and should be used only in particular circumstances. You may notice that only a subset of maybe the most vocal children participate.

Pros	Cons
• Good for basic tasks involving simple interactions and gathering information. • Good when led by an adult or very competent child. • Work well when quickly split into sub-groupings to come together with work at a later point.	• Not good for activities involving discussion, planning and decision-making tasks. • Talk on a single topic is very difficult. • Shy children will not get involved. • Free rider effect and diffusion of responsibility are very likely.

Case study – group-size problems

Ms Kaur wanted to use group work in her class on a collaborative task where pupils would identify and decide on the rules for group working. After briefing the class she split them into four groups of seven pupils. This resulted in:

- Some pupils doing little work, messing around and disrupting the group and class.
- Groups splitting into sub-groups: one to do the work; the other off task.
- Pupils interrupting and talking over each other.
- The topic of conversation drifting, often going off task.

The experience was very frustrating for pupils; there were many confrontations and many of the more able, conscientious pupils developed an immediate dislike for group work. Smaller groups of three to four pupils would not have led to the host of problems experienced. If pairs had been used to start the task, perhaps as a brainstorming exercise, and then fed into groups of four, which evaluated and edited the list, then the exercise would have been more productive and less frustrating.

The number of groups

The smaller the groups, in terms of their size, means more groups to be monitored. In order to focus your attention on one particular group, all other groups should be able to work without your constant attention. A teacher is less likely to give full consideration and help to a particular group when multiple groups are dependent on him or her for low order procedural questions and support. If the number of groups poses a particular problem, you could think about having only a few groups working at a time while the remainder of the class works individually. However, it might be worth persisting since your teaching and management load should ease as pupils develop confidence in their group-working skills.

Group stability

This aspect of group functioning is often overlooked. Groups go through stages in their development. One well-known sequence is 'forming, storming, norming and performing'. These stages are meant to follow each other, though with new challenges groups can revert to forming and storming modes. However, the longer the group has been running, the less likely this is to happen.

Maintaining stable groups from the second week for at least a full term or a semester enables pupils to overcome insecurities and conflict by developing relationships, trust, respect and sensitivity, and encourages them to participate and contribute to group activities. (We provide more information on this in the next chapter.) If groups are changed too early or too often, then trust building may have to be restarted. *Don't treat conflict as a reason to change the group* unless it is severe. Children need to learn how to work with others regardless of who they are. Learning how to resolve interpersonal as well as learning problems is a key outcome of effective group working.

Stages of group development

Tuckman (1965; for full reference see p. 94) identified four stages of group development:

- 'Forming' – children are unsure of each other, trust is low, insecurity and uncertainty are high, children are highly sensitive, few may contribute to the group work, one child may dominate.
- 'Storming' – conflicts and disagreements increase, cliques form, clarification of goals begins. This all indicates increased safety and is a necessary part of the trust-building process. Supportive conflict resolution strategies are needed. Personal conflict is to be avoided.
- 'Norming' – increases in satisfaction, safety, trust, tolerance of conflict, consensus and compromise, groups become more task orientated and cohesive. Conflict is managed more effectively.
- 'Performing' – increase in productivity, performance and quality, planning, problem solving and discussion.

Case study – stable groups

Mr James had always changed the groups for different activities for a variety of reasons. He felt that stable groups were unnecessary since the class generally 'got on' and the pupils were not difficult. Furthermore, the Literacy and Numeracy strategies in England required grouping by ability, which meant that changing groups was necessary.

He decided to try stable groups for all subjects. After some initial conflicts, pupils settled into their groups and group work. They became much more proactive and worked harder. Most pupils seemed to enjoy the work and also began to support each other informally when they were not doing group work.

Teachers' views – on group stability

This year I really tried hard not to swap people out of groups because the ones who managed to stay together without any interruptions tended to work better as the year's gone on.

(Teacher 3, School 4, P9)

One of the things you said after the initial meeting was that pupils might want to change after a term. I did try that but I think they were better staying in their groups.... I went back to that [stable groups], I found it was better. Because they'd already got this relationship and were used to taking turns.

(Facilitator 1, School 4, P5)

Group composition

Group members will not always get on with each other. As a teacher you will need to pay attention to the types of conflict that may be observed in group working. A difference in perspective (as in problem solving) is often productive. But if you can limit personal conflicts, you will maximise the potential for learning. On the other hand, it is unrealistic to think that you can avoid all personal conflicts. However, incidents that lead to these conflicts can be useful in the development of group-work skills by reviewing and reflecting upon the conflicts with your children during debriefing (see next chapter).

Allowing children 'free choice' in the composition of their groups can reinforce social divisions (e.g. same gender and ability) and isolate children who are not chosen (especially those with disabilities). Children can, however, be included in the selection of *criteria* for determining group composition. This allows pupils a say but reserves the decision for the teacher. A number of key composition criteria that can affect the effective working of groups are considered below. Fundamental to these criteria is the consideration of pupil grouping as 'inclusive' or 'exclusive'. Inclusive grouping allows children to work (and form positive relationships) with all types of children in the class – mixing ability/attainment level, gender, friendship, disability, etc. Exclusive grouping brings together children who are of similar ability/ attainment, sex, friends-only, etc. This grouping practice can help to provide differentiated material/tasks for children but it may also become the basis for children to stop interacting with anyone who is seen as 'different' from themselves.

- *Ability or attainment grouping[1]* – This is a controversial topic. Some teaching and learning strategies recommend same-ability groups, but this is often for classroom management rather than for social learning purposes. Group work necessarily involves a certain amount of mixing students by attainment. On the basis of a number of studies, it is recommended that any small grouping of children should not include the extremes of high and low attaining children. *We suggest that it is best to put together high to middle attaining pupils, and low to middle attaining pupils*. This reduces pupil frustration due to large differences in understanding while maintaining some inclusion across the attainment range in your class. Higher attaining pupils benefit from working with lower attaining pupils because they are encouraged to explain what they know/think, which helps firm up their own knowledge. Similarly, lower attaining pupils get to know about new ideas and ways of thinking.

A teacher's view – on mixed attainment groups

I'm thinking about L, who is low ability, if I were to put him with two other low ability children, they would never have the ability to include him and ask him the questions and think about things beyond themselves, but because he's with middling, quite good children actually, although that can be frustrating for them, they're also able and mature enough to say 'and what do you think?' and 'can you see?' and 'why don't you do this bit?' So there's possibly a problem there, isn't there, if you've got a low achieving child with other low achievers, that actually nothing very much would get done at all. So it's quite a balance, isn't it?

(4 Teachers, School 4, P2)

- *Gender mix* – An equal balance of each gender is best to encourage contact between the sexes and to prevent one gender dominating the activity. Same-gender groups may be more effective when boys or girls tend to dominate materials or the work, for example, working on a computer (usually boys) or scribing (usually girls).
- *Friendship groups* – Another controversial topic. *In practice, it may be best to balance friends with non-friends in a group.* Friends can work well as they know and (usually) trust each other, and they are better able to manage any conflict that may arise. But friendship pairs do not always work well in situations where children must help or tutor each other. Care is needed, as some friends may tend to engage in off-task behaviour, particularly boys. This can be exacerbated when the class has a negative view of group work or when the task does not challenge students or warrant group work. Also, children's friendships can be 'stereotypical', as friends are often of the same sex and attainment level. So if you want to promote inclusion in your classroom, you should think beyond the convenience of friendship as the basis for grouping.
- *Personality and working style* – Some pupils have conflicting personalities or may not work well together. Some children may disrupt activities, and solitary or very quiet children may hinder the group. *It is important to stop personality types dictating the success or failure of groups.* These difficulties can be used to good effect by encouraging children to speak, to learn how to deal with different colleagues and learn not to dominate the group. Children should be encouraged to work in groups whatever their personality type.
- *Integrating children with special educational needs (SEN), English as an Additional Language (EAL), or isolates* may be difficult – A child may contribute little without particular support or cause conflict between group members. However, learning to work with particular individuals can greatly benefit a

group. Many schools try to promote inclusion in their classrooms, and a key way this can work is through the inclusion of pupils with SEN and those for whom English is an additional language in as much group work as possible. Inclusion carries a twofold value here: it helps pupils with SEN or who have EAL to learn group-working skills that will enhance their learning and motivation in the future, and it will help other members of the class to adapt their expectations and friendship preferences to include these children. Be warned, though: this type of inclusion does not happen over night – it takes time for everyone in the class to adapt their group-working skills for inclusion. You need to be particularly careful about the role of Teaching Assistants; they are too often left to work with a group of low attaining pupils and those with SEN, and this group can become separated from the teacher and their classmates. Teachers who persevere with the inclusion of children with SEN in group work, however, report that effective inclusion of, for example, children with autism or emotional or behavioural difficulties is possible, with classmates taking responsibility for inclusion rather than relying on the teacher. Initially, careful consideration and group-work development are required in order to decide into which groups these children should be integrated. It may be helpful for the group to receive some supportive coaching (see Chapter 7) in the form of encouragement of positive attitudes and positive ways to involve the child with SEN. In some cases the child with SEN may need some constructive support and advice to help him or her integrate into the group work activity. These might be part of briefing or debriefing (see Chapter 5). Other suggestions for including children with SEN are included in Chapter 11 on troubleshooting.

For children with English as an additional language, some teachers suggest putting same primary language speakers together. Invariably this means they communicate in their own language which can provide necessary support but may not sufficiently challenge the child. At other times it is useful to put a child with EAL with a sensitive, helpful partner who can only speak English and who can take the time to explain things. It might be useful to be very clear about the sorts of things the partner should do: explain what words mean (to develop vocabulary), try to rephrase things, etc. It is important to recognise that children with EAL and/or SEN do not always need to be actively involved in the group, they can and do benefit from listening and observing other peers in the group. Nevertheless, it is important that these children do feel part of the group and attend and engage with their peers.

Teachers' experiences and ideas on integrating pupils with special educational needs

One group of teachers we worked with explored with us the range of difficulties that they had experienced involving students with SEN into group working activities and the range of approaches that they had used to overcome these difficulties. It can be a frustrating experience because there are no straightforward solutions, not least because these children vary so much in terms of their needs. Some children with SEN can struggle to participate within the group while others can react negatively to group working. Similarly, other group members may not react kindly to including children with certain types of need. Our group of teachers highlighted much value in thinking carefully at a more strategic level of where you want to get the child with SEN and the group to in the long term as well as thinking about the particular arrangements for a group work task on that day. For the particular context it is important to consider for both group and the child with SEN the level of challenge posed by the activity, the size of the group and the nature of the interaction between group members. These elements should not all be challenging at the same time.

A child with SEN can become more involved within a group if positive attention within the group and class is drawn to the particular skills that they do have and how they can contribute to the success of the group work (i.e. giving them a positive role relative to the activity/group). Alternatively, it might be useful to consider encouraging and possibly training or coaching one or two individuals within the group in strategies to support and actively include the child with SEN. This will benefit these children's skills and learning as well, but these children need to be selected carefully in terms of their maturity, skills at engaging in a supportive way and self control. It can be useful to have children with SEN work with just a partner at other times, and for particularly challenging partner-work tasks, they may be part of a triad and thus able to observe the other two members interact (though care is needed because triads can create tension and frustration). Sometimes children with SEN (and others) may choose to opt out of group work, and it can be useful for them to see and realise the fun they are missing out on by doing so.

However you choose to involve pupils with SEN or EAL, this issue needs careful thought and flexibility to ensure that the group members are sufficiently challenged without them having to take on too much. Groups may need some individual support through coaching (see Chapter 7) in thinking about how they can be inclusive, involving and supportive. They can also be encouraged through briefing and debriefing to reflect on how they can resolve any difficulties with inclusion that the group members are experiencing in the future. Many of the practices outlined in the troubleshooting chapter (Chapter 11) relate to some of the difficulties that can arise when trying to include pupils with SEN and it would be worthwhile reviewing these.

Think about ...

- How could you best set up the classroom to enable you to switch quickly between whole class, individual and group work?
- Group size - some pupils may be more confident and capable of working in larger groups (of four or five), while others may be more confident beginning with partner work.
- Do you need everyone to participate? Perhaps working in pairs will help increase participation. In using pairs, teachers can frame questions such that each child needs to report on their partner's thoughts.
- How you will integrate particular pupils? With whom will the SEN, EAL and 'difficult' pupils work best? How will you adapt arrangements for more challenging activities?
- How you will react when children say they want to change groups? At what point should you let them do so?

Note

1   The term 'ability' is problematic in many ways. Strictly speaking, a child's 'ability' is not easily assessed but the term is often used to represent perceptions of ability in an area based on performance on one or more attainment tests and/or on the teacher's professional perceptions of a child's achievement and 'potential'. In this book and consistent with other literature on this subject, we will use the term 'ability' to mean these things rather than a definitive notion of a child's ability.

Chapter 5

Developing pupils' group-work skills

Pupils need to be prepared for group work. Before groups can work productively, children have to be positive about working together and they must feel safe and secure in each other's company. Such feelings of safety involve pupils:

- feeling comfortable in dealing with differences and confrontations;
- believing that their ideas will be listened to and respected; and
- having the confidence that they will not be embarrassed, rejected or exposed for expressing their ideas and views.

Encouraging feelings of safety and security requires what we call a 'relational approach'. This stresses the need for pupils to have the social skills to engage with each other sensitively while trusting and respecting each other. They also need to communicate effectively by listening, explaining and sharing ideas, and should be able to plan, organise and resolve problems during their group work. These skills will help them work more autonomously, be less dependent on the teacher and engage actively in learning. Group-work training activities are organised around a relational approach structured into a developmental sequence, with an emphasis on *social skills*, followed by *communication skills*, leading to more *advanced group-working skills*.

The approach that we recommend throughout this handbook emphasises the development of positive, secure and confident relationships, such as those with a parent or close friend. This approach allows pupils to develop the social skills which facilitate the development of children's responsive communication skills and allows them to engage with new problems confident in their ability to work with others. It serves as the basis for group-working skills described in this chapter (and the suggested activities in Part II) and is organised into a developmental process where more advanced skills build on earlier skills. It also promotes interaction and inclusion of children. The relational approach assumes that all children can develop their group-working skills together, initially by reorienting the classroom from focusing solely on curriculum content to include a focus on relationships. Remember, it takes time for children to develop group-working skills. Sometimes the class may be eager to move ahead and at other times the children may need to take a step back to reinforce their trust and communication skills before they can move forward again.

A teacher's view – on fostering group working skills

There are certain skills in group working that maybe before you just assumed that putting children in a group they'd get on and work without spelling it out for them. I think this is really spelt out [in the programme]. It's important to take turns. It's important to look at each other. It's important to share jobs. They're made aware of it really. That's the difference, they're not normally aware of those things. We've made little cards with group rules on and put them around the table and say 'this week this activity – you on this table, I want you to concentrate on not fiddling, or looking at each other', or whatever it might be. We'd never have done that before. We'd have just done the activity, not thought about how they were going to do that activity – that's quite a big difference.

(Facilitator 2, School 4, P2)

Preparing pupils for group work

For group work to be effective, pupils need to understand what it involves and why they will be doing it. Some children may believe that they have little to learn from each other. Time is therefore needed at the start to talk about how and why group work is useful and to give pupils the opportunity to contribute their thoughts and ideas. Pupils should be given the chance to develop a shared set of ground rules for their group work at the outset, and given time to review and further develop these ground rules over time. They also need time, before and after each group-work session, to participate in 'briefing' and 'debriefing' relative to their developing group-working skills. Briefing discussions may focus on the particular skills that pupils might use in a task or possibly particular group challenges that might come up during the course of a group activity. This briefing period should prepare them in thinking about how they will do these skills in practice and how they will manage these challenges. Briefing is also the time to explain the need and use of the activity to be undertaken. A period of debriefing after the activity provides pupils with the opportunity to reflect on what they have done, why it worked and what improvements can be made. Once children understand why they are doing group work and what is expected of them, they can begin to develop their group-working skills.

A teacher's view – the importance of briefing and debriefing

The strongest thing for me was talking through with the children how and why the group worked or whether we'd met that specific group objective. That's the bit which is the hardest bit to adopt in some ways.... . It's actually talking through the aspects of group work with the children.

(Facilitator, School 5, P2)

What do pupils bring to group work?

It is helpful for the teacher to try to empathise with the way in which children experience group work and how it feels for them to work with other members of their class. Many pupils may have mixed feelings about group work; some will enjoy it; others may find it frustrating and slow. Engaging in group work can be hard and emotionally wearing, especially for younger children. Children are keen to get their own way and do not necessarily have the skills to reach a compromise or to let insignificant issues go. It is thus important for you to be prepared for this, to anticipate that some children will be upset or frustrated, at least in the early stages of undertaking group work, and to plan accordingly (it might be helpful to review Chapter 7). Try to put yourself in the children's shoes and remember that:

- Each child brings different experiences of working with others. Whether good or bad, these experiences will influence involvement in and enjoyment of group work.
- Without group-work training, children may express a preference to work only with friends.
- Group work can leave pupils feeling insecure and unsure since they want to please the teacher and to get the work 'right'. This can discourage them from developing their own ideas and they may display reluctance to engage without adult guidance.
- The more schooling children have experienced without developing group-work skills, the more difficult it may be for them to undertake these new practices.

Part of genuinely understanding and empathising with what children experience during group work is to give them a voice, and provide a safe and supportive group environment where they can reflect, communicate and share their experiences. The relational approach has been structured with teachers and pupils to help overcome feelings of threat and insecurity that often prevent group work from being a successful or enjoyable experience. We think that it is essential, therefore, to work with your class as it develops through the sequence of social and communication skills towards advanced group working. As your children are developing these skills, it is helpful to start small and build up group work gradually.

We recommend simple activities that take place in a safe and secure environment; often it will be helpful to ask children to work in pairs. Once they have gained confidence in undertaking activities as pairs, you can begin to undertake similar activities in small groups of three to four pupils. (While the sequence and structure of the relational approach are described here, recommended activities are found in Part II.)

Motivating pupils to be effective group workers

If you make it as a challenge, don't you find if you say, 'This is a really difficult activity, it's going to be so hard to do this because you're going to be very tempted to be silly, but if you try your absolute best' ... and say, 'Many adults would find this difficult' – if you build it up and build it up, they really rise to that ... and I was thinking, it's just to do praise isn't it? Because it's just massive amounts of praise and making it a challenge for them.

(4 Teachers, School 4, P5)

Advice from teachers.

Social skills

Pupils need to be able to develop close, supportive relationships with everyone in the classroom – not just with preferred friends. Social skills help build up an understanding of what is involved in being a member of a group as well as the confidence to work openly with others in the group. Important social skills are:

- trust
- mutual tolerance
- mutual respect
- sensitivity to others

Leading to

- positive self-esteem
- self-confidence
- ability to deal with conflict

Activities designed to develop social skills encourage pupils to see situations from other people's perspectives. These activities are productive in building positive relationships between pupils in the group and are thus helpful in advancing group development. If the group membership changes, then it is useful to go back through some of these activities to redevelop the relationships.

Communication skills

Effective communication skills have to be developed and supported. These skills help pupils communicate with each other and think about their ideas through the use of explanations and joint reasoning. As they develop, children improve in their expression of feelings, become sensitive to each other's feelings and thoughts and become more able to handle complex thoughts and ideas.

The features of group talk which are indicative of effective learning are:

- taking turns to speak;
- active listening;
- asking and answering questions;
- making and asking for suggestions;
- expressing and requesting ideas and opinions;
- brainstorming suggestions, ideas and opinions;
- giving and asking for help;
- giving and asking for explanations;
- explaining and evaluating ideas;
- arguing and counter-arguing;
- persuasive talk; and
- summarising conversations.

A teacher's view – on explaining skills

I think there is always the element, if you're explaining something to other people, to actually put it in a language that will convince them is actually developing greater clarification in your own mind. If you teach something to someone ... you become clearer in your own mind what it is.
(Teacher 2, School 6, P3)

Advanced group-working skills

Advanced group-working skills help children work together to overcome problems of difference in perspective and to organise themselves effectively so that they are less reliant on adults. This will encourage children's autonomous learning and responsibility for their own learning. Moreover, in many group-working situations, pupils must have higher order thinking strategies for tackling complex tasks. Some advanced group skills are:

- making group decisions and coming to consensus;
- compromising;
- encouraging all group members to become involved; and
- planning the group work, which consists of:
  - working out the timescale;
  - deciding whether an activity or understanding prior to group working is needed; and
  - deciding whether to use roles within the group or to allocate aspects of the task to different members.

Developing pupils' group-working skills over a lesson

Pupils learn best when they are given opportunities to reflect on and then adapt their group-working skills (see figure below). This encourages children to take responsibility for their own learning and to become active in the development of their own skills. We have found that each group-work training lesson should consist of three main phases within which certain activities should take place: briefing, group work, and debriefing.

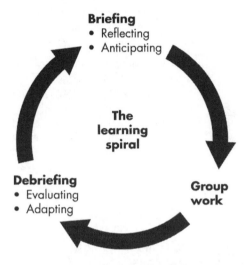

Briefing
- Reflecting
- Anticipating

The learning spiral

Group work

Debriefing
- Evaluating
- Adapting

Briefing

- *Reflecting* – Discuss a particular skill such as listening, as a class or with partners/groups. Identify *what* needs to be improved or the class should reflect back to the previous group-work lesson (see Debriefing).
- *Anticipating* – Ask pupils to identify *how* they will put this improvement into practice, what they will do. This is very important because we often know what is going wrong but not what to do in order to resolve the problem.

Advice from teachers.

Getting the best from briefing

What I found helped ... for all of them actually, is to give them ... before an activity to give the group something, one of those rules to concentrate on, just to keep them focused on that thing, that helps. Even if they've just got one. Sometimes you can give two, but mainly just one is enough to keep them concentrating on some particular aspect of working with a group. I find that does help.

(Teacher 1, School 4, P6)

That's what I found useful as well. Because there are so many skills for them to remember, but if they know they're particularly concentrating on taking turns or particularly concentrating on eye contact, or not fiddling, whatever it is, they can manage that, then they feel they've achieved something as well, don't they. They feel positive.

(Teacher 2, School 4, P6)

Group work

This is where children experience group work. To help pupils focus on the skills they are to learn (identified during briefing), the teacher should remind the pupils about the behaviour they are expecting during group work. This can be written on the board under the heading 'What I'm Looking For' (WILF, described in Part II), with verbal reminders throughout the lesson.

Debriefing

Debriefing provides pupils with the valuable opportunity to reflect on what they have achieved together and how they have worked in their groups. This can help the teacher evaluate how successful the session and group work were. If pupils are to present the outcome of their work, this should be done prior to the debriefing.

- *Evaluating* - Groups discuss/individuals think, 'How well did we/I do?', 'What do we/I need to change in order to improve?'
- *Adapting* - Pupils discuss evaluations and how their group work can be improved in the future. Stop children from being overly personal or critical.

Pupils should be encouraged to focus their discussion on the processes within their group: for example, feelings and emotions within the group and what, in their opinion, could be changed and improved. Here pupils have the opportunity to talk about their experience and reinforce positive impressions as well as bringing into the open any unpleasant feelings. Through reflection on their own experience and listening to each other, pupils can develop a deeper awareness about themselves, the group and the group-work process.

Briefing and debriefing are both very important, as this is where reflective learning takes place. *If opportunities for reflecting and evaluating do not take place, then the learning spiral is broken and children may not progress.* It is common for debriefing to be omitted because of lack of time. If this occurs, start the following lesson with a debriefing (maybe as part of the briefing). Without opportunities to anticipate and reflect on their developing skills it is likely that some children will not improve their skills and the benefits of group working may be more slowly realised. It may even be instrumental in creating negative attitudes towards group working. This three-phase format (briefing – group work – debriefing) should be used for all the training activities but also, from time to time, when group work is used in the curriculum (at least once per week). Debriefing should not just be used for troubleshooting. It is important that pupils get opportunities to recognise what went well during group work and why as well as to identify and discuss the reasons when things do not go so well.

When is debriefing important?

You would probably take your lead from the children. If you had a particularly successful lesson where you really notice the children working well, you might discuss that at the end, or else at that point if children are falling out and weren't working well together you'd probably think 'well I need to talk about this' and we'll have a whole session on this next time or we'll talk about it now. I suppose you take your lead from the children. If it's all working smoothly, perhaps you just let it go [Authors' note: though you should praise pupils when it has gone well and review with them why it went well].

(4 Teachers, School 4, P3)

Advice from teachers.

Case study – practise what you preach

Ms Fernandes had been using the SPR*in*G programme of social and communication skills activities for about half a term. She noticed that her pupils were able to talk at length about how they *should* behave and interact when working as groups during the briefing part of the lesson. However, she also noticed that they would rarely behave in these ways when working as groups.

Pupils were treating the briefing, group-work and debriefing parts of the lesson as completely separate contexts and not developing their group-work skills. With effort Ms Fernandes began to bridge the gap between saying and doing by reminding pupils to focus on specific group-work skills while they were actually doing the group work. She also encouraged pupils to think about *how* they could do the skills and behave in practice and *how* they could improve the particular skill when they next did group work.

Boundaries for group work

Be clear with the class about the 'rules' for group work. For example, during briefing and debriefing, not mentioning others' names, using the 'I' message (how it made me feel).

Advice from teachers.

Think about ...

- How you can integrate the relational skills training into the curriculum and weekly timetable.
- How you can support and facilitate the development of positive relationships within groups and your class outside of the training activities.
- How you can ensure that pupils reflect on and positively adapt their group skills in the light of their group-work experiences.
- How you can make sure that pupils 'practise what they preach' and behave in the ways they say they should.

Chapter 6

Creating effective group-work activities and tasks

Teachers and other adults in the classroom are fundamental to the development and support of effective group working. There are a number of roles and activities that teachers and other adults can undertake to support groups.

How can I best organise group-work activities?

A main way to plan for group work is by setting up each group in such a way that pupils feel safe about contributing to the group as well as planning the task so that it is challenging and legitimises group work. Developing safety within groups is part of the relational approach described in Chapter 5. Insights into how you may set up and support activities and tasks are considered here.

Creating well-organised tasks that encourage group work

Designing tasks that encourage group work is challenging. *It is important that the task is set up in a way that encourages all members to talk and work together, and does not encourage individual working.*

Case study – too many materials

Miss Hanif wanted groups of four children to work together through a number of mathematics problem-solving questions. She gave each child a sheet containing questions with spaces for the answers.

The result was a complete absence of discussion and four separate, and often different, answers to the questions in each group. Despite having told pupils to work together, they had worked alone. Had Miss Hanif given a single answer sheet to each group (and one question sheet), then communication between group members would have been encouraged.

A single task output

The more possible outputs there are, the more likely it is that the group will divide. It is important that groups work on a single output. One good strategy, therefore, is to give the group only a single sheet of paper on which to write or prepare their output (though tasks should not involve one member writing for lengthy periods while others just watch on, as this leads to disengagement; they too need to be involved in another element of the task). Groups should also be given no more than a single copy of the instructions. Of course, if the group is expected to split into sub-groups to do sub-tasks, then multiple sheets of paper and pens will be needed.

X

✓

Advice from teachers.

Using a single set of materials

I think it's counter-productive if the task is such that people in the group feel that they're not doing anything. That ... [can be] the case when it comes to the paper-and-pencils tasks. When there's paper and pencil for one between four, others can be left not doing anything, even though you can take turns. But then there's also the boorishness of writing things down, other people barge in, tell a joke or something, the work loses the impetus. It can work, I did some nice posters last year with the Year 5 and on the whole I think it does work much better with just one pencil [and a single sheet of paper].

(Facilitator, School 5, P4)

Allow time for group planning

Pupils like to get on with things. In order to encourage them to plan their group work it may be necessary to withhold resources for a few minutes to allow them to organise themselves and discuss how they will do the task. Otherwise, pupils tend to jump ahead and try to get the work done before they have planned what they are going to do.

Designing different types of task

The point of group work is to get children talking and explaining ideas to each other. This means they are *actively thinking*. It is important to make sure that the task involves much more than simple activities such as cutting up pieces of paper or writing the answers to simple sums. If tasks solely focus on such low level practical skills, then the potential for group work will not be realised.

The task should be challenging for pupils, yet not too difficult. Tasks that are high in *ambiguity*, where the outcome and/or the path to that outcome are not obvious, are challenging. Ambiguity raises the need for reasoning and thinking and when conducted in a group setting leads to discussion, shared reasoning and debate to solve problems and make decisions. If ambiguity is too low, then group members know what they have to do and how to do it, talk and high level discussion may not be required and learning may be limited.

Tasks can also vary in terms of how *open ended* they are. Some have a single right or wrong outcome (closed), some multiple correct solutions (albeit with some solutions better than others), and some are open-ended tasks where the outcome cannot be judged as right or wrong (though they may be of better or worse quality).

Some ideas for creating open-ended tasks

- Ask questions where there are no clear right or wrong answers: for example, 'How can we make the school a nicer place to be?'
- Set an activity where the group must create something (e.g. write a piece of fiction, prepare a play, create a work of art, musical composition, etc.) given one or more criteria or constraints.
- Ask a question where there are a number of possible solutions but groups have to weigh up strategies in order to decide which solution is best or most correct.

Some ideas for creating closed tasks

These tasks have a single right or wrong outcome. A good closed task would be where groups have to think through and discuss the various strategies to reach the correct solution: for example, identify a strategy for getting across the playground without stepping on the ground or devise a means for calming the traffic around the school. Discussing the different possible answers to a multi-choice question might be a poor group task.

Different types of group interaction

Group-work activities can also vary in terms of how children *work together*:

- Coordinating interaction – where pupils coordinate their actions by working on different aspects of the same task. They may take turns to do an individual gym routine, collecting and recording information, group-work roles, etc.

- Cooperative interaction – where pupils share information, experiences, views, opinions and explanations, instructing others, helping, etc.
- Collaborative interaction – where pupils work intellectually together to solve problems, make decisions, plan their work, analyse, synthesise and evaluate.

Tasks should be chosen on the basis of how demanding they are for pupils. Simple activities that require children to coordinate their efforts are a good introduction to group-work activities. Tasks that require children to cooperate either by sharing information or by helping and explaining ideas to other pupils are a good second step. Complex tasks may be best introduced as paired work. Once effective communication skills are developed, collaborative activities should be more frequent. Collaboration is most effective in developing and supporting high level learning and understanding.

Structuring the group-work activity

The group-work activity can be structured so that children focus on a single goal or activity at a time. This structuring of the group work supports groups that are not yet able to plan and carry out the work as a whole. Group work can be structured:

- by splitting the task into *sub-activities*;
- through *snowballing*; and/or
- by giving pupils different *roles* in the activity.

Sub-activities

There are multiple ways of structuring group work into sub-activities. This involves the teacher dividing the task into a number of more manageable, yet coherent, sub-activities and then guiding groups through each sub-stage of the activity.

Time deadlines for the end of each sub-stage encourage groups to knuckle down and get on with the activity (i.e. time pressure). Verbal reminders may be needed, especially when the duration of the task is lengthy. However, if deadlines are too strict, they can make children feel that they are never allowed to finish anything, that the teacher does not trust them and that they do not own the work.

Splitting a task into sub-activities

- Group debate: group brainstorming (to identify the main issues) → group discussion where the issues, reasons and counter-arguments are exchanged (to apply/extend reasoning and understanding) → feedback to class.
- Solving a problem: group brainstorming (to collate possible ideas) → evaluating reasons for ideas → deciding which idea is best → applying idea.
- Group research: plan research → individuals research and learn material → share it with others → write it up as a group.
- Group experiment: make predictions and explanations → test predictions → discuss implications → prepare group report.

Snowballing

Tasks can be broken down into sub-activities and accompanied by sequencing the size of groups: for example, moving from individual work to dyads and then to groups. This is called 'snowballing'.

Snowballing ensures everyone engages in some thinking rather than relying on others to come up with ideas. It is good for discouraging 'free riding', particularly when it begins with individual work.

Snowballing in a science experiment

1 Individuals/pairs make predictions and explanations.
2 Group (of four) shares and discusses ideas to form group predictions.
3 Test predictions as a group.
4 Discuss implications as a group.

See Chapter 9 for further ideas.

Once pupils improve at group work, you should begin to encourage them to plan the overall activity themselves (especially group research and experiments). Initially this can be conducted as a whole class where a joint decision is made about how the task will be approached and conducted. Eventually groups should be able to take responsibility for planning their work themselves. The teacher should also encourage pupils to take responsibility for keeping their work to time.

Roles

Roles can be allocated to group members to encourage a feeling of group responsibility or, for instance, to prevent the same person (often a girl) from doing all the writing. However, *roles must be used and selected with care*. It is important that all group members are *equally* engaged in the collaborative exercise. One problem occurs when 'timekeepers' do nothing but watch the clock and do not engage in the substantive aspects of the activity, such as the generation of ideas, group reasoning and discussion. Similar problems may arise when spokesperson, group encourager and other roles are introduced. Allocating roles is probably best used when pupils are experienced at group work, but some basic roles can be introduced early on (e.g. scribe, chairperson and spokesperson). It is important that children know what the role involves in practice. Time spent discussing roles or identifying a role description is fruitful (see Part II). Teachers should initially consider identifying which child should adopt which role but once children are able to take more responsibility, allow them to decide who will take on each role. Identifying a particular role for children with SEN or EAL that enables them to successfully contribute and makes the most of their skills can help ensure they are included in the group activity.

Case study – successful task structuring

Miss Abbot wanted to use group work in her class for a collaborative decision-making task where pupils decide on the rules for group working.

After briefing the class, she encouraged the pupils to brainstorm in pairs as many rules as possible without evaluating them. After ten minutes, pairs came together into fours and compared and evaluated their rules. They then selected the five most important and general rules. After fifteen minutes, they fed these rules and the reasons for them back to the class and spent the remainder of the time deciding which five rules they would use as a class.

Miss Abbot found this worked very well, especially as children were able to collate some ideas in preparation for the group work. This meant that even those children who rarely contributed to group work had something to add.

Think about ...

- How you can design tasks that encourage children to work together rather than go their own way.
- How you can structure a lesson into a set of sub-activities that help pupils do their work more autonomously.
- How you can gradually implement time deadlines so that pupils can begin to work together more efficiently and, if need be, under pressure.
- How you can ensure that pupils take on particular group roles as well as their normal responsibility to contribute to group work.

Chapter 7

The role of the teacher and other adults in supporting group work

Adults can adopt a wide range of roles in supporting group working. However, *the notion of the teacher as the holder of knowledge which is to be transmitted to pupils is inconsistent with the benefits of group work*. Under these circumstances, pupils are prone to become passive learners and are less likely to think for themselves or take responsibility for their own learning.

How can I support pupils doing group work?

In order to get the most out of group work, adults in the class need to *support and encourage* the group's attempts to do the task rather than direct the group how to complete the task.

Being a 'guide on the side' rather than a 'sage on the stage'

One of the main aims of group work is to encourage pupils to take responsibility for their own learning, and thus be less reliant on the teacher as a source of ideas and direction. More support is likely to be needed in the early stages of the development of group-work skills. But try to decrease your intervention in group working gradually and encourage pupils to maintain the group work themselves. The adult's role is therefore to:

- *circulate* and *monitor* groups rather than working with one particular group;
- *guide* groups when they encounter difficulties;
- *model* and *reinforce* good social and conversation skills; and
- *coach* individual children and groups in cooperation skills.

As your pupils become more competent in their group-working skills, you will find it easier to assume these roles. The children will become less dependent on you for direction and support, allowing you to act more effectively and reflectively in these roles.

A teacher's view – adult control of group activity

A lot of teachers will feel that they want to control it. It is difficult to let go. Teachers, especially class teachers, are in control, and they are guiding everything and I think that's the most difficult thing, letting go, letting your children do it.

(Facilitator 1, School 4, P8-9)

Circulating and monitoring groups

Monitoring involves spending more time listening to what the groups are doing rather than intervening. This may be very difficult at first, as many children like to be told what to do and adults like to keep children on task. Stick with it for a few weeks, though; children and adults will soon get used to it. While you are monitoring, note the positive and negative examples of group working, the amount of equal participation or the level of explaining to each other, so that these incidents can be discussed during the debriefing part of the lesson. However, on occasion, intervention will still be necessary (e.g. to re-explain instructions, to prevent misbehaviour, to resolve conflicts or to get a group back on track).

There are three circumstances when it is useful to intervene in groups: (a) when group members are unsure about what to do or how to do it; (b) when group members are having problems communicating with each other (for example, they are not explaining their reasoning or questioning the explanations offered by other group members); and (c) when one or more group members dominate the group work. Monitoring the group interaction before rushing in to help is important and will help establish the nature of the group's difficulties and the potential questions to ask or assistance to offer.

Guiding groups

The teacher (and any other adults in the classroom) will need to support the group and intervene when necessary. This can be accomplished through a *guiding* approach: working with pupils and groups in a way that encourages them to think for themselves and act responsibly. When asked explicitly for help, adults should think about making *suggestions*, giving *explanations* and asking *open-ended questions*. Try to avoid being overly directive or acting as a giver of information since this can lead the group to be less productive. When helping a group it is important for the adult to work from the pupils' ideas and thinking, and thus connecting the help offered to their thinking. Effective support from adults involves the use of questions to probe pupils' thinking and to encourage them to make this explicit as well as to clarify ambiguous points to other group members. Adults should avoid offering up their own ideas or telling children how to do something or what to consider as this encourages pupils to be more passive and to accept these views without question. Adults supporting groups can *suggest* possible alternative ways of thinking or alternative considerations (e.g. saying things like 'Have you thought about alternative ways of doing that?' or 'I wonder, have you thought about trying it this way?'). What is important in terms of the given support is that it is closely related to pupils' thinking about the task and the strategies they are using to undertake the task.

Supporting groups

When supporting groups, to clarify what they've talked about, if you're in the group supporting them, making them stop and just make a note or agree with what they just talked about so that it makes it clear in their mind what part they're up to in the discussion.

(Teacher 2, School 5, P1)

Some children need me to remind them. I'm not sure if I haven't gone over and said 'Is everyone having a turn?', 'Why don't you ask him what he thinks?' whether they wouldn't have done that naturally. They're still very egocentric at this age; they're not very able to look around at other people in the group particularly. But with encouragement they will.

(Facilitator 2, School 4, P2-3)

Advice from teachers.

Modelling and reinforcing group-work skills

Adult intervention ought to be to the point and conducted in a way that *models* and *reinforces* good social, communication and group-working skills. Focus on talk strategies that are positive and inclusive: for example, 'What do you think?', 'Why do you think that?', 'What's your view?', 'That's a good point', 'I think this because ...', 'Yes, but ...' and so on. The teacher should also model and reinforce skills during briefing and debriefing as well as during whole class teaching or lessons that maybe do not involve the use of group work. The point here is that this is about developing a form of communication and discussion within the class where pupils are required to explain and clarify their thinking, their reasoning and problem-solving strategies both during group work and during class discussions.

Case study – becoming a 'guide on the side'

Miss Costa was trying to do more group work in her class. However, she was frequently frustrated by pupils' passivity: they remained very dependent on her support and assistance.

When observed by a colleague it was noticed that her interaction with groups was very directive and that she wanted the children to do the task so well that she had begun imposing her ideas on them. When this was highlighted she changed her approach by encouraging pupils to work things out for themselves and to find independent ways of getting the required information – through books and by asking other pupils for help and their views.

Initially, the pupils were resistant to this approach, which was very stressful for Miss Costa, who considered abandoning the whole project. But after some time the children settled into the new way of working, they became much more independent in their thinking and learning and they began to enjoy group work much more.

A coaching role

The teacher (and other adults in the classroom) can also take on a *coaching* role to help develop pupils' social, communication and group-working skills. This may involve advice to an individual or a group (e.g. to help encourage them to involve another group member or to reduce the dominance of one pupil). You should evaluate current group-working skills and problems encountered and think together about how they can be developed or resolved. Again, the more that new strategies can come from the pupils, the better.

A teacher's view – a coaching role

On the whole I've left them to their own devices to sort out their roles. There was a girl ... who was very bossy, but very good at organisation, and she got very frustrated. I put her in a group of people that were not responding to her bossiness and she was getting more and more frustrated.... I took her aside and said 'Look, you're really good at organisation but you're just telling people what to do and they don't like it, so you've got to say to them things like, "You're very good at that, so you do that", so you can get everyone to do what you want, but you're doing it in a more subtle way'.... It's a skill. You're going to come across people who don't do what you want to do, but you've got to learn how to get them involved.

(Teacher 2, School 6, P4)

Teaching Assistants

In recent years there has been a massive increase in Teaching Assistants and other paraprofessional workers in UK schools. Though less extreme, this increase is happening across many other countries, too. The largest study so far on the impact of TAs found that the more support pupils received from TAs the *less* progress they made at school in mathematics, literacy and science. There are several reasons for this, but a main problem is the way that TAs are deployed in classrooms: they are often assigned to work with low attaining pupils and those with SEN, sometimes in the classroom and also supporting out of class interventions. The problem with this arrangement is that these pupils then become separated from the teacher, the curriculum and their classmates. Pupils with SEN in mainstream UK schools, for example, tend to spend most of their time with other low attaining pupils and those with SEN. Some TAs do a great job of course, but there is also a tendency for TAs to stress task completion and the feeding of correct answers to pupils, which is at odds with pupils becoming independent in their work and the kind of group work we are stressing in this book. Sometimes TAs can dominate groups, not allowing pupils the freedom or time to discuss with each other. The deployment of TAs is therefore an important factor in the experience of group work of certain pupils in classrooms, and teachers have a responsibility to look carefully at how they use their TAs.

TAs can work with groups in ways described in this chapter – that is, they can take on a monitoring, guiding, modelling, reinforcing and coaching role – but it is important to stress that the teacher has the responsibility for making sure that the TA is clear about the goals of the group-work activity, and needs to be aware that the TA should not dominate group work, or emphasise task completion over task understanding. One way to think about this is to ask how the TA can *add value* to the teacher's contribution, for example, by providing a previously arranged monitoring function for a group, and then later feeding back to the teacher information on how pupils worked in the group. This can be done while the teacher works with another group, or is involved in another activity. Another way to make good use of TAs, and avoid the common situation where TAs only support the low attaining pupils or those with SEN, is for the TA to work with the higher attaining pupils, thus freeing up the teacher to work with these other pupils. Alternatively the teacher and the TA can rotate their involvement with groups, so each group gets to work with the teacher and the TA.[1]

Think about ...

- How you can model good group-work talk and interaction.
- How you can maximise and support pupil contributions during group work.
- The types of indirect intervention (guiding) that are most helpful to avoid pupils remaining dependent on your directions, questions and answers.
- Carefully monitoring the deployment of TAs to ensure that high quality group work is available for all pupils in the class.

Note

1   Readers interested in knowing more about the TA role and ways in which they can maximise the impact of TAs might find it helpful to look at the book: *Maximising the Impact of Teaching Assistants: Guidance for School Leaders and Teachers* (Rob Webster, Anthony Russell and Peter Blatchford, 2016, Abingdon, Oxon, UK: Routledge).

Chapter 8

Evaluating group work

Our experience of working with teachers and pupils has led to the identification of a number of classroom actions that indicates when group work has been successful over the year. These are some of the positive characteristics of pupils who experience effective group work identified by teachers who have been working with us:

- Shared ownership of learning tasks and responsibility for behaviour and learning
- Increased feelings of safety, security and equality with each other
- Strong relationships built within the group and across class
- Increased tolerance of peers
- Increased mutual respect for peers
- Positive working environment
- Improved speaking, reasoning, compromise and questioning skills
- Thinking independently
- Cooperative problem solving
- Supporting and helping each other
- Increased ability to get on with their work with minimum teacher input
- Increased inclusivity when socialising with peers
- Increased participation in discussions (in groups and whole class)

How can I evaluate the success of group work?

Group work needs to be continually evaluated so that you can take steps to resolve any new or ongoing problems or issues. Problems generally fall into the following key areas:

- Group arrangement and ethos
- Group interactions
- Role of adults
- Activities and tasks

We have included a 'Teacher evaluation of group work' *pro forma* worksheet/form at the end of this chapter that will help you and your colleagues assess the success of group work. You should use this from time to time to review how well children are progressing in their group-work skills and to reevaluate the arrangements and functioning of group work. It is important to also reflect on how the arrangements or experiences of group work might be improved further. The example form provided could be used by other teachers or staff members (see Chapter 10) to review group work in your classroom and to provide an alternative perspective. To be used effectively, this should involve a positive and constructive process, and the evaluation could feed in to a whole school monitoring of the implementation of group work across the school.

The evaluation form provides a general review of issues and ideas that we have covered in the first seven chapters of this handbook. If you are unsure about the meaning of any of the 'Aspects to look for', a quick review of the earlier chapters will help. After assessing the group work in your class, it may be useful to refer to the troubleshooting chapter (Chapter 11) or to review your plans for preparing and supporting group work (Chapters 4-7).

How can pupils evaluate their own group work?

We have also included two sheets that enable groups and individual children to evaluate their own group work. Self-evaluation encourages pupils to think about how they can improve their group skills. These sheets should be used on a fairly regular basis, especially during training. The evaluations should relate to one specific piece of group work that the children have done recently. You could, on occasion, ask a child to observe groups working and use the questions on the sheet to guide the observation - however, you must ensure that feedback is constructive and used in conjunction with briefing and debriefing aspects of the Learning Spiral (see p. 41). It would be worthwhile discussing the feedback an observer will be providing to a group or groups to ensure that it is constructive.

How can I assess group-work outcomes?

Assessing children individually can be problematic when work is carried out as a group because individual assessment can encourage competitiveness rather than cooperation. It is more constructive for group-work outcomes to be assessed at a group level or, if individual marks are still to be awarded, for them to be combined to give a group score. The latter can encourage peer helping within the group as it works to increase its score by supporting those individuals who may be weaker. You could ask groups to mark each other's outcomes. Some teachers have asked groups themselves to agree on how a group mark should be divided among individuals. Great care is needed when doing this, as it can lead to arguments and blaming but it can be useful to get pupils to think about this before the group activity takes place.

Assessing group work

Two questions - 'How is it working?' and 'How can it be improved?' - should always be at the back of your mind.

Advice from teachers.

Suggested evaluation sheets for teachers and pupils

Teacher evaluation of group work	
Aspects to look for	Comments and notes
Group arrangement and ethos • Does the furniture arrangement allow group members to interact? Can it be improved? • Can everyone see everyone else? • Are group members close enough to each other to hear and talk quietly? • Do children in groups lapse into smaller sub-groups (e.g. more talk in pairs than to the group)? • Is the group size appropriate for the activity and does it enable all to participate? **Group interactions** • Are all group members involved in the talk and work (i.e. no one dominates, is shy or free rides)? Can this be improved? • Is the majority of talk on task? • Do group members show good active listening skills? • Do group members take turns at talking (e.g. do not interrupt or talk over other people)? • Does group discussion involve pupils reasoning and debating together? • Do group members question each other's ideas (e.g. to clarify, to elaborate or to get reasons)? • Is the group able to reach a consensus or compromise? • Do group members respond positively to each other? • Do group members provide supportive and constructive feedback? • Is the group able to resolve petty arguing? **Activities and tasks** • Do resources/materials encourage group work rather than individual working? • Was the task structured to support group work (e.g. snowballing, task phases, jigsaw groups [see p. 70], etc.)? • Did the task encourage pupils to discuss together/interact? **Role of adults (Teachers, TAs and other adults working in the classroom)** • Was the group dependent on the adult(s) for completion of the task? • Did I/adults encourage pupils to manage their time? • Did I/adults brief and debrief pupils about working in a group? • Did I/adults give pupils an opportunity to evaluate their own group work? • Did I/adults remind pupils to use their group-work skills during the activity? • Did I/adults monitor (listen without intervening) group interactions? • Did I/adults guide pupils by asking them open-ended questions, making suggestions, etc. (rather than telling them)? • Did I/adults model good interaction skills? • Have I/ adults given the pupils opportunities to do group work in the curriculum?	

How well did we work as a group?

Group name: _____   **Date**: _____

Discuss each question with your group. Tick the box that shows how your group feels about how well you worked together. **Make sure you all agree on the group answer**.

Question	Yes	Some yes/ some no	No
Did everyone get involved in the group work?	❑	❑	❑
Did everyone have a chance to share their ideas?	❑	❑	❑
Did anyone encourage other people to offer ideas?	❑	❑	❑
Did everyone explain their ideas?	❑	❑	❑
Was everyone's contribution considered fairly?	❑	❑	❑
Did anyone ask questions if they did not understand?	❑	❑	❑
Was everyone happy with the final group decision/outcome?	❑	❑	❑

Write down any ways in which you think you and the rest of the group could work better together next time.

1 ....
....
....
....
....

2 ....
....
....
....
....

3 ....
....
....
....
....

My involvement in group work

Name: _____   **Date:** _____

What I did that helped the group work well	What I did that hindered the group from working well
What other people did that helped the group	**What other people did that hindered the group**

How can I improve my group's work?

....

....

....

How do you think you and the rest of the group could work better together next time?

....

....

....

Chapter 9

Using group work in the curriculum

The activities outlined in Part II of this book are designed to help you train your pupils in social, communication and advanced group-working skills. These training activities will be useful only if pupils also have regular opportunities to reinforce their skills and engage in group work in other parts of the curriculum. Once pupils have received some group-work skills training and have become familiar with evaluating and adapting their skills, group work can be used much more regularly within different parts of the curriculum. This chapter offers suggestions for developing and implementing your own group work within the curriculum. A variety of ideas and examples are offered of different types of group work suitable for both short sessions and longer sessions that may be conducted over several lessons or even a term.

How can I start using group work in the curriculum?

When you begin to introduce group work across the curriculum, remember to keep group sizes small (e.g. pairs), up to a maximum of five pupils for more complex activities. It is our experience that group work can be used in all curriculum areas, and every effort should be made to use it on a *regular* basis in the curriculum. This will allow pupils to get used to group work as a form of learning and provide opportunities for them to further develop their social, communication and advanced group-working skills.

Group work is most effective when it is used to *encourage supportive communication and high level talk and reasoning*, rather than when it is used for activities like collecting, sharing and presenting information. Engaging in high level talk may be difficult for children in KS1, but young children (even at the preschool level) can still benefit from cooperation, sharing ideas and helping each other, providing a basis for more advanced forms of group work. In fact, it may even be easier to initiate and develop group-working skills with young children, as they will have had less engagement in traditional, individualised classroom activity. Children may engage in more complex forms of group work if they work in pairs and the task is structured as a series of clear steps. You may be surprised at how well even young children can work as a group, as long as they have the appropriate group-working skills.

In this chapter and in the activities in Part II, we indicate the suitability of each group-work structure for different-aged pupils in the tinted heading that appears before each description. We have distinguished between **lower primary** (children aged 4 to 7 years), **upper primary** (children aged 8 to 11 years), and **primary** (children aged 4 to 11 years).

Group-work activities

Once groups are ready to engage in group work in the curriculum, some basic forms of group work can be used. Later, these simple forms of group work can be strung together to create structured but more complex forms of group work. Finally, more open-ended group projects and group debates can be used. We describe these various forms of group work with regard to their contributions and drawbacks, and provide some curriculum-specific examples. These curriculum descriptions may be extended and applied to other subjects in your class.

PRIMARY

Quick group activities

Designed to last no more than five minutes and can be conducted during a whole class interactive session. The most efficient way to do short-term group work is to use pairs (e.g. talk partners or think–pair–share) to brainstorm ideas/facts, to share knowledge, for one child to help another on a particular activity or to engage in joint problem solving.

- Pros: Encourages thoughtful involvement and equal opportunity (as opposed to whole class interaction, where some individuals switch off). Quick and efficient to use.
- Cons: If the question/activity is not focused, this approach can lead to confusion or off-task chat. If too little time is given for a question to be explored, then learning can be inhibited and confusion reigns. An individual child can dominate.

Examples

- English: To draw out current knowledge at the start of the lesson, *brainstorm* examples of types of words or phrases – prefixes, suffixes, metaphors, similes.
- Science: To speculate, predict, explain – get children to *problem solve* – for example, why the moon appears to change shape from a crescent to a disc.
- Mathematics: To compare different strategies and/or explanations for answers to particular problems – for example, assign one or two multiplication problems to pairs and have each pair discuss how they calculated their answer before reporting it to the rest of the class. If partners do not have the same answer, encourage them to explain why their answers are different.

Collecting information

Small groups are given a task where they must collect, collate and pool information. The group may divide up the task so that each member has a different job or different area to research and thus some group planning is required.

- Pros: Good for developing basic group-work planning and for giving pupils experience of how to carry out particular jobs or procedures. Good for practising research skills.
- Cons: Pupils may learn only about what they have directly worked on. High level thinking, discussion or explanations are unlikely to occur unless there is synthesis or evaluation of the information collected (e.g. what the data means or how it relates to a theory). The best extension is to get the group to discuss, analyse and evaluate the information they have collected and then write this up.

Examples

- Mathematics: To examine the concept of probability, get groups to roll dice a number of times and to note down the sum of the numbers. They can produce a tally, graphs and so on.
- English: Group members read separate chapters of a book or separate poems and then pool their information in relation to a particular issue, summarise the chapter, and so on.
- History: Group members may study separate sub-topics of a topic (e.g. writing, lifestyle, clothing and education of the ancient Egyptians) and then pool this information to make a group report.
- Science: Pairs or groups have different powders or sponges and pour water on to their materials. They look closely using hand lenses, monitor and record what they see happening and discuss ideas about bubbles rising. Their collective views and information are shared with other pairs or groups.

Sharing information

Pupils present knowledge/ideas/experiences about an issue or topic to the rest of the group (or class). This may require some prior (individual or group) research before it takes place (e.g. see the Collecting information section above and the Jigsaw groups section below). Best used when individuals/pairs collect information on a specific sub-topic of a group topic and then share this with the rest of the group.

- Pros: Allows groups to gain a cursory understanding of a topic or piece of information. Encourages the person doing the sharing to have a good understanding of the topic.
- Cons: Pupils may not listen unless tested afterwards. May lead to surface understanding of the main ideas but little depth in understanding or actual

experience. Does not allow for high level discussion or shared reasoning unless followed by group discussion.

Examples

- Mathematics: Talk partners – one pupil explains to another how they would go about answering a maths problem.
- Cross-curricular: School council representatives report back on a school council meeting. Pupils share experiences of their holidays.
- English: Pupils share summaries and evaluations of the books they have read recently and explaining their thinking in the process.
- History: Pupils report back to a group on their research of a sub-topic that is relevant to the group topic (e.g. ancient Egyptian writing, hieroglyphics, education, buildings, etc.).

Peer helping

Helping can be used best in mathematics, science, PE, computing and other areas that are more factually and procedurally based. The focus is on pupils explaining to each other about *how* to do something.

- Pros: Useful when time or equipment is limited. Allows one-to-one guidance and the pair work at the novice's pace. Can lead to good understanding of procedures in both novice and expert.
- Cons: Helping requires good understanding and ability to explain logically. The quality of help given can vary dramatically. Helpers may need training in breaking down a task into smaller steps.

Examples

- Mathematics: Pairs of children work separately on similar problems (e.g. alternate maths questions). They then come together and swap the problems they have worked on. The expert then guides the novice through the process of tackling the problem. (See also Setting problems for others to solve, p. 69.)
- Cross-curricular: The teacher explains to a group of pupils how to do a task (e.g. use a protractor or computer software). Experts develop and pool questions/problems for the novices to work on (and maybe to test them). Each expert is paired or grouped with a novice/novices and must explain to them how to do the task.
- English: More able children can support and help the less able with their reading.
- Science: Experienced children can explain to novices about how to use particular pieces of science equipment. The very advanced could explain to others about what needs to be considered and how to carry out a fair test in science.
- Physical education: Ball skills. One child supervises another while they both practise the skill, followed by how to integrate it into a series of movements and extend it.

Collaborative creation

Pupils are brought together in pairs or small groups to work together to create something new. This can be anything from writing, music or art to drama or PE. Particular criteria, themes and materials can be used to limit the open-ended nature of the creation. This form of group work may require planning on the part of pupils, especially when groups coordinate jobs/roles and collaborate in their activity. Pupils enjoy this form of group work as it allows them autonomy in the nature of what they do.

- Pros: Allows pupils autonomy, encourages creativity, planning, sharing ideas, explaining through high level discussion and carrying out of the work.
- Cons: Can be time consuming. Some members might not participate; others might dominate. Children can be overambitious.

Examples

- Music: To create a piece of music using instruments (maybe that the children have made) that sounds like certain everyday activities (e.g. the path of a drop of water to the sea, a production line, a train or the tension in a story).
- English: Write a poem that uses alliteration, simile, metaphor, onomatopoeia or is in a specific form.
- Dance/science: Create a dance performance that expresses thunder and lightning.
- Art/design: Produce some artwork in a particular genre or style, or as a response to a shared experience.

UPPER PRIMARY

Group debate

Pairs or small groups explore and explain differing views on a particular topic. Pupils should be encouraged to present different views, examine the reasons for them and address these views with counter-arguments and explanations. While pupils are not expected to come to a consensus or agree, they should try to persuade each other of their different views. They can, of course, agree to disagree.

Pupils do not just engage in discussions on issues that directly affect them or about which they are familiar. They can learn about, and then discuss, other issues. Under these circumstances, research and an open mind are needed, and the process may take much longer to collate the evidence and then to have a debate.

- Pros: Encourages depth in understanding through high level talk and reasoning as well as analysis, evaluation and synthesis of ideas, concepts and explanations. Pushes pupils to persuade others, consider alternative ideas and change their own views.

- Cons: Can lead to heated arguments and fallings-out. May be too complex for young pupils. Can be time consuming unless good research resources (if used) are available. Some children may dominate while others take a back seat.

Examples

- Geography/PSHE: Groups debate particular issues – hot topics (e.g. fox hunting, immigration), moral dilemmas and curriculum-relevant topics (e.g., traffic-calming measures, the value of recycling, etc.)
- Cross-curricular: Structuring a debate – one pair from a group collect information in favour of a view, while another pair are against. They then listen to each other's arguments in favour and against, collect further information to counter these views and present again. Finally, the pair that looked for ideas in favour of the view must present the arguments against the view and the other pair that collected ideas against a view must present arguments in favour. For example, groups argue the case for the benefits of being a Spartan or an Athenian in ancient Greece.
- Religious education: Learning from religion. Groups have to find out what different religions teach about vegetarianism. They have to weigh up the rights and wrongs and prepare an argument one way or the other to present in a debate.

PRIMARY

Group problem solving and decision making

Pairs or small groups are given a task where they must work together to solve a problem or make a decision (e.g. on a course of action). Some tasks may be closed (pupils may know what they have to achieve but not necessarily how to achieve it, and this is what they work on), while others may be much more open-ended (e.g. what to buy with school resources). Collaborative group work may benefit from a preliminary round of brainstorming or individual work that can feed into the group discussion.

- Pros: These tasks often call for higher-order thinking and reasoning, and thus may be very beneficial for critical thinking and learning. The activities thus involve applying knowledge, synthesising, analysing and evaluating ideas.
- Cons: Can be time consuming, depending on the activity. Some members may dominate, be left out or free ride. Arguments may arise, making consensus difficult to achieve.

Examples

- Science: Children speculate or brainstorm individually (or in pairs) on a scientific question before discussing the question as a group. For example, which of a number of objects will float or sink, and why?

- Cross-curricular: Planning an investigation or project. Planning what information from a project to write up and present to the class. Deciding criteria on which to review other pupils' written work.
- Mathematics: Children discuss which mathematical operations to use to measure the area of the playground or the volume of an odd-shaped classroom. A more specific question might be: 'How many 2.5-litre bottles of cola will fill a 25m × 3m × 5m swimming pool?'
- Citizenship/cross-curricular: Deciding which group made a better case for a particular hot topic. For example, whether ball games should be allowed on the playground. Or which is better, being a Spartan or an Athenian (see above)?
- ICT: Prepare a presentation, Web page or prospectus for the school.

Group projects/investigations

Group projects or investigations usually involve stringing together some of the basic group work structures. For example, group decision making (planning) → collecting information → sharing and analysing information → sharing analysis with the class. Numerous combinations are possible. Projects and investigations will take time and planning, but will extend pupils' understanding of the curriculum.

- Pros: Allows pupils a lot of independence and autonomy and thus are enjoyable. Encourage planning, depth of understanding and use of lots of skills, including high level talk, reasoning and explanation. Ideal when planning a scheme of work over a half term.
- Cons: Some members may not pull their weight. Unless adults provide a supporting role the group may get drawn in the wrong direction. Unless timing is carefully monitored by the group the task can take longer than expected.

Examples

- Science projects: Develop hypotheses, plan and carry out a test, analyse the results and write up and/or present the findings.
- Science and design and technology projects: Utilise findings from science work to identify practical ways of improving particular products – for example, using a balloon to power a toy car, friction to slow down objects, micro-environments, etc.
- English: Prepare different articles for a class newspaper.
- History: Research houses and housing in the locality. Using different source materials, children research information about how houses and housing have changed over time. They select and organise historical information so that a corridor display can convey their findings to a wide audience.

UPPER PRIMARY
Other combinations of group work

Many combinations of group work types are possible. While there is something to be said for simplicity, a number of structures are very useful. Here are some examples.

Individual brainstorming → group-work thinking and decision making

This is very useful as it encourages all children to engage in some preparation and thinking prior to engaging in a discussion, ensuring that everyone does a bit of work and has something to contribute.

Examples

- Science: Encourage pupils to make predictions and explain their reasons about what will or will not happen – for example, what will and will not grow and why.
- English: Brainstorm persuasive words to use in a flyer to drum up support for an issue or to act on an issue (e.g. lobbying the headteacher to extend lunchtime play).
- Religious education: Explore the meanings behind signs and symbols of a range of religions. Class brainstorms ideas about signs and symbols they know, sharing information. Groups collect information about the signs and symbols of different world faiths. They note associations with times of the year when these signs and symbols are incorporated into rituals. Groups use this information to design a symbol to convey something that children commonly identify with and feel plays a significant role in their lives.

Setting problems for others to solve

Brainstorming → decision making → problem solving → peer helping

This combination uses a variety of different types of group working strung together to give a powerful learning situation which is particularly useful in maths. It is also useful to do Stages 1–3 alone.

1   Devise problems in pairs.

2   Pass problems to next pair along line.

3   Pass problems back to original pair for marking.

4   One member from the pair explains to one member from the other pair where that pair went wrong.

5   Pairs reform and one child explains to the other where he or she went wrong.

Jigsaw groups

Collect information → share information → peer helping/share information → group report

1   Used where the class studies a main topic (e.g. pollution, recycling) in which there are a number of sub-topics (e.g. car pollution, power stations).
2   Groups of four each research a specific sub-topic. The group may have a large pile of books and each person can skim through a couple to get as much information as possible on the sub-topic and then feed it into the group. The group becomes *expert* on the specific sub-topic.
3   The group is then split up and each expert member becomes a member of a new group consisting of experts who have studied different sub-topics. Each child *shares* (teaches) what he or she has learned with the rest of the group. The group (or individuals) write a booklet/report on the overall topic.
4   This can be followed by an assessment on the overall topic, and group scores are given based on the sum of individual scores or lowest individual score. This encourages experts to make an effort to explain (teach) what they have learned to their group, and equally the group will make an effort to learn (please note great care is needed when marking groups and individuals – see Chapter 8).

Examples

Pretty much any topic can work as long as there are sufficient resources (books, access to research resources) and the area is of a level that children can understand.

• Geography: In studying local land use, group members can be assigned sub-tasks to research surrounding hills, rivers/oceans/straits, urban areas, rural areas. Once each member has information on a particular area, the group comes together and each student reports findings to the rest of the group. Alternatives could be studying of different elements relating to pollution, global warming, recycling, etc.

- Science: Different types of bones, species of insects, animal lifecycles, etc. – more reference-based work is good for this type of group work.
- Art: The life and works of a specific artist and their different styles of artwork, methods, or the approaches of different artists working within a genre, etc.
- History: Fashion, money, society, justice, education, etc. in a certain historical era or civilisation.

Other useful combinations

Brainstorming (group) → evaluating reasons for ideas (group debate) → deciding which idea is best (group decision making)

This may be used to plan a group project, or what to do in a collaborative creation or as part of a problem-solving exercise.

Learn/research material (individuals/pairs) → share it with others (groups) → write it up/test each other (groups)

This format could be used in research sub-topics of a group topic (e.g. humanities subjects). Groups learn the material that individual members have collected and then are tested and write everything up as a group or even in individual reports.

Plan investigation (group decision making) → collect data (group collection of information) → analyse data (group debate) → discuss implications (group decision making)

This format would be typically used when conducting a science investigation from start to finish.

Predict and explain (individual thinking) → discuss predictions and explanations (group decision making) → test predictions (groups collect data) → discuss results (group decision making)

Also could be used in science to formulate hypotheses and discuss understanding of the science concept under study.

Chapter 10

Developing a whole school approach to group work

The most efficient and effective way of implementing the ideas in this handbook is to do this across the whole school and therefore schools should strongly consider adopting a whole school approach to the use of effective group work. This means that children can build and develop their social, communicative and advanced group-working skills year on year. We have shown already that group work can be used effectively with the youngest pupils of age 4–5 years in school; starting this young means that in later years group work becomes routine, less disruptive and easily adapted for specific curriculum areas. It also means that the school staff build a culture of sharing and collaborative development in practice. It is not always easy for an individual teacher to introduce new ideas into their classroom if they do not have the support of their colleagues and a common purpose. It is much more effective if colleagues can share their experiences; plan together; where possible, observe each other's classrooms; and share feedback experiences with colleagues. These practices can be a very worthwhile part of school improvement more generally.

There is another good reason why a whole school approach to group work is important. Schools are in the business of helping children develop skills that will serve them in the immediate and long-term future. Effective group work is a main way that schools can enhance some of these important skills. Not only can group work help children learn key social, emotional, and communicative skills, but group work provides important experiences in team working, group problem solving and decision making, conflict resolution, planning activities as well as confidence in engaging with peers and supporting pupils that are less able and/or more able than themselves. In many senses group working can furnish children with the 'soft skills' required to succeed in school and work environments after formal education. When managed at the whole school level, it can help with the development of responsible behaviour and moral development. This is a rationale for group work that is different to its benefits for individual academic attainment, but just as important.

What follows is a consideration of the key elements that need to be in place in order for a whole school approach to effective group work to take hold and develop within a school.

School senior leadership responsibilities

Perhaps the single most important part of a successful whole school approach is that it has the full support and involvement of the headteacher and the senior leadership team. They can create the necessary conditions to ensure that group work extends from policy through to practice and that it is effectively implemented, supported and monitored in classrooms. It is also important that a key person takes on the support and facilitation of the work to be undertaken across the school and that time is made available for staff to attend within-school training. Making time and space within the timetable and within the curriculum to undertake group work training, possibly as part of lessons on personal, social and moral education, is also important for successful implementation.

We should be under no illusion that implementing group work right across the whole school takes time, possibly even a year or two, to really get it working properly and a further year to reach sustainable levels. The senior leadership team should plan for this.

There are a number of key things that schools can do in order to enhance a whole school approach to group work. The following sections outline the important overriding elements that need to be in place for a whole school approach to group work to succeed.

Incorporate effective group work into school policies and development plans

We recommend that schools and headteachers make effective group work part of the school's teaching and learning policy and their development plan and that the ideas expressed in this book are used as the basis for work across the whole school. This will provide the impetus and will lead to the sustained use and further development of pupils' group-work skills as they move from one school year to the next.

Identify a group-work facilitator and champion

We have found that one important way of enhancing implementation of the ideas in this handbook across the school is to identify a senior staff member to take responsibility for facilitating and championing group work. It is the facilitator's role to coordinate implementation and to ensure that the use of group work and the development of group-work skills training are sustained across classes. We have learned from experience that it is vital that the facilitator is a member of the senior leadership team or at least is clearly supported by them; allocating this responsibility to a relatively junior member of staff can render the initiative less effective and can sometimes make things difficult for them. Another strategy is to have two staff members to take on this role who then work together to facilitate the use of effective group work across the school (possibly each one taking a different phase of education). This has the added benefit that if one person leaves the school, the skills, knowledge and impetus do not also go.

The group-work facilitator would have a primary role in:

- becoming an expert on group work;
- encouraging staff to implement the ideas and practices recommended in this handbook;
- encouraging staff members to think about when and how they can implement training and group working in their classrooms, initially aiming for training and group work to take place at least twice per week;
- ensuring that group work is planned for and regularly discussed by teachers (e.g. in planning and staff meetings);
- facilitating the sharing of effective practice among staff groups;
- modelling effective group work and training activities for other staff;
- monitoring the implementation of group work and training by class teachers across the school; and
- providing feedback on implementation and how group-work practice might be improved.

Ideally a facilitator would have first-hand experience of setting up and implementing group work with pupils in the school. It is worth the facilitator taking some time to try out the ideas in their own particular classroom before facilitating their use across the school. A key part of the role is likely to be fielding questions relative to the possible difficulties that can arise with group work, especially in the early stages, and suggesting helpful strategies for overcoming these problems. Implementing a whole school approach requires persistence and determination on the part of the staff member responsible. It is also very useful if the facilitator has time to support teachers in their classes and to monitor, through observation, implementation.

A teacher's view – the importance of a facilitator

What worked well? I think the way it's been planned. It's needed somebody to give the information, to act as a reference and to be able to demonstrate. It's having someone who's confident; who understands the process. And it's the whole timetabling of it that has worked very well. And I feel by putting it on a timetabled schedule, it's shown our commitment towards it. From the Head's ... profiling of it, 'This is really important, we're going to make it work' and having that from the start prevented any worries, panics of timetable or scheduling.

(Teacher 1, School 6, P1)

Establish in-service training and regular planning meetings

A main way of providing an impetus for the implementation of effective group work across the school is to introduce the key principles and practices within a half or full day of in-service training. Within such an event teachers and teaching assistants can try out some of the activities themselves, they can do group work and learn to reflect on and evaluate their group work. This session really needs to sell the idea of group work to teachers and to present the positive effects that it can have in terms of enjoyment, effects on personal, moral and social skills, behaviour and on learning.

Implementing group work as a whole school approach

You need to sell it to them [teachers] and they need to own it and they need to feel it's something they really want to do. And they're doing it because they feel it will be worthwhile for the children. You've got to do that with them ... and you say, it has come from the top. And the Head's both very keen on the idea and sees the benefits of it because we do lots of other things as well. I think that's very important, it's got to be seen to come from the top – and then people have got to feel they want to do it as well. Sell it to them, get them to own it.

(Facilitator 1, School 4, P9)

Advice from teachers.

If in-service training time focuses on group work at one or two points over the year then teachers and staff can develop their skills, share their experiences (successes and failures) to enable them to move forward. They can also use this time to develop a plan for implementing group-work training.

This training session and a follow-up can be used to get group-work training and implementation started but in order for this to be sustained, other structures need to be in place. It is important for small groups of teaching staff to meet regularly to plan, discuss, give feedback and problem solve together in relation to group work in their classrooms. This may be something that teachers that normally get together to plan their teaching and curriculum coverage do or it might become an add-on to departmental meetings. Either way, these groups of teachers need to take some ownership of the implementation of training and group working and plan for this together.

A teacher's view – regular staff meetings

We found it worked well because we had staff meetings every three or four weeks and regular updates and feedback. Possibly that person's time, your key worker or facilitator as such, your SPRinG representative, they need time out to be able to be in other classes, and it would make it work even better, to do the modelling role [model the approach].

(Teacher 1, School 6, P2)

It would be worth creating a special slot in these planning meetings to discuss the practices and activities (including new ones that you have found or developed) connected to group work. These small groups of teachers could also use video in their classrooms to capture what groups do, how teachers and TAs work with groups, and so on. This can be used to self-evaluate, help solve problems, share and develop practice and to get positive and constructive feedback from colleagues.

Ensure opportunities for group-work training in class timetable

Ensuring that there is a regular slot in the weekly class timetable allocated to the development of group-working skills is an important way to ensure that the whole school approach to group work is carried right through into classrooms and is sustainable. Ideally this would be for between forty-five minutes and one hour but even thirty-minute training sessions might suffice. Setting aside this time for group-skills training can make things easier for busy teachers and makes sustained and successful implementation of group working more likely.

It is also important that teachers try to plan for and use some form of group work within the curriculum as part of everyday lessons. At first this may be once or twice a week but this should increase as teachers and pupils become more confident in engaging and supporting group work.

Implementing a whole school approach: lessons learned

Some schools that we worked with tried an approach that involved integrating group-skills training sessions into the day-to-day coverage of the curriculum. There were thus no special lessons devoted to training in and thinking about group-working skills. On the face of it, this seems like an efficient way of combining group-work training and curriculum coverage. In reality, this did not work. Teachers rarely had the time to think about how to bring training and the curriculum-focused activity together, and thus training sessions became sporadic. When group-skills training did take place, this element was rushed and the curriculum-focused learning objectives would take precedence over group-skills objectives. The all important briefing and debriefing elements that are so central for the development of group-working skills were often left out. This meant that implementation of group-skills training and group working never really got going.

We also found in the course of our research that some staff would go along with the programme but not really commit to implementing it or adopting the principles and activities in full. Some teachers would only utilise the training activities very intermittently, often without briefing and debriefing. We came to call this 'SPRinG Lite'. It could be manifest, for example, in only doing a group-work training activity perhaps when there was a little time left over at the end of a day, assuming the main curriculum areas had been covered earlier. This was to misread the way in which group work is best integrated into the work of the school. Group work, we believe, is not an add-on to the real work but a main way in which the real work in schools can be achieved. The development of group work as part of a whole school approach creates a culture within which 'SPRinG Lite' is minimised.

Schools and teachers need to implement the programme in three main ways: first, by creating space in the timetable for group-skills training; second, by adopting and thinking about the principles and practices outlined in Chapters 4–7; and third, by making regular efforts to bring group work into lessons so that it becomes a main way of undertaking curriculum-focused class work that complements other approaches to teaching and learning.

Suggested plan for implementation into the school

These are some of the features that will enable a whole school approach to group work to be successful and for its huge potential to be realised in the school. It is important to keep in mind that adopting and implementing such an approach can take some time to take hold in a school. It is likely that during the first year there will be a number of complications that arise. Teachers that are new to the classroom or that lack confidence will need support and encouragement and those that like to control or micromanage children's learning may need some guidance on relaxing this control and letting the pupils have a go at doing group work. As one of our teachers suggested, 'Implementing group work can require a bit of a leap of faith'. Pupils may also have some difficulties adjusting to a new way of working. Asking children to work together inevitably brings some social tensions to the fore but with time, training, experience and support they soon adapt and begin to enjoy it and value learning much more.

We suggest the following stages to implementing group work within the school:

1   Facilitator is identified.
2   Phase 1: Facilitator works with one class over a period of time, maybe a year, to test group-skills training and the recommended practices in Chapters 4 to 9.
3   Phase 2: CPD/ in-service training sessions led by the facilitator enable group working to be understood and implemented by other school staff.
4   Create time during staff planning meetings to discuss group-work implementation.
5   Create time within the class timetable for group-work skills training activities.
6   Encourage staff to adapt lessons to incorporate increasing amounts of group working.

While implementation of the whole school approach takes place there will also need to be regular efforts to monitor and evaluate the success of the implementation. This will provide useful feedback for thinking about how to adapt implementation as well as useful evidence to establish how worthwhile it all is. This allows the facilitator and the school to take stock on how to improve things, but also enables the facilitator to improve the support for teachers, support staff and pupils to improve their group working. So the two final stages relate to such monitoring and evaluation.

7   Monitor the use of group work and pupil and teacher experiences over time.
8   Evaluate the success of group work over the course of a year and a phase in school.

Advice from teachers.

Implementing a whole school approach

What we found has worked well was timetabling from the start, so from the introduction at the start of the year ... and we worked through the book in a number of staff meetings, three or four, where we each had to go away, read a section by a certain time, have completed this element, carried out that element, carried out this activity, and also it's allowed for feedback and therefore Mr X [facilitator] could go in and support classes who were having difficulties with it or have any questions. So we got the whole theory about it, we understood it and we actually participated as a staff in the activities, that was really helpful, actually doing it yourself... . We had a big support at the start where we most needed it, and then classes have gone on to work with it.

(Teacher 1, School 6, P1)

Monitoring and evaluating the implementation and impact of effective group work

We should be under no illusion that by implementing effective group-working strategies there will be immediate and obvious effects on pupil attainment. Why would there be? Group work is just a different, albeit more powerful, means to an end. It is important to remember that the effects of group working take time to happen and they may be more subtle than first expected. Children need to develop and then make use of the skills for any effects to occur. For example, changes might be expected in terms of the way children work together, with more engagement and less free riding, more argument initially and then later turning into more discussion, children may become more supportive; they may be able to express themselves and their ideas more coherently, they may be able to evaluate evidence more effectively and so on.

Teachers' ability to support, facilitate and question pupils may also improve relatively gradually. This means it is important to monitor and evaluate both the process of implementation and the effects of the whole school approach to group working. There a number of ways that this can be achieved by the facilitator in conjunction with teachers and pupils in the school.

There are several evaluation sheets in Chapter 8 that can be used to monitor the implementation and the effectiveness of the whole school approach to group work. The teacher evaluation sheet might also be used by the facilitator during a classroom observation while group work is taking place. The completed evaluation can be used to support and provide constructive feedback to the teacher and other staff regarding the group work in their classroom. This evaluation sheet might be completed at two to three points over the year by a facilitator or by teacher colleagues to provide a range of perspectives as well as insights for these persons to see how group work functions in different classroom contexts. Similarly, the group and individual pupil evaluation sheets might be used to inform the facilitator about how well children are progressing and that they are setting themselves challenges for improving their own group-working skills.

It would also be useful for teachers to keep a record of when they do group-work training and when they utilise group work in the curriculum. This can then be linked to performance and progress data that may be collected within the school. But it is important to remember that the use of group work in one curriculum area is not going to have a generic effect on performance, certainly not at the start, though it may do so as pupils build on their group-working skills year on year and utilise their skills for joint thinking and learning.

At the end of the year it will be important for the facilitator and senior management team to take stock and to adapt and improve, where necessary, the approach to the implementation of training for and use of group work in subsequent years.

Chapter 11

Troubleshooting

Resolving common group-work problems

Introduction

In working with teachers over a number of years, we have encountered and overcome a number of problems concerning group work. Below, we provide examples of problems and offer ways to overcome them. In addition to the specific recommendations, we remind readers that many group-working problems may arise from lack of trust and support among group members. As we recommended in Chapter 5, the relational approach (developing social, communication and advanced group-working skills) underlies effective group work. When children encounter problems working with one another, it may be useful to draw upon/ return to fundamental trust and communication activities to reinforce group solidarity and stability.

Group members do not practise what they preach

Children are often very good at telling you how they should act during group work but often do not behave in this way. This is an important issue to overcome since it is the *doing* of the group-work skills that we are trying to change.

We can get around this problem by emphasising the main skills that are to be learned and practised throughout the lesson but particularly when *briefing* the practical activity. Most important is following up and discussing how pupils can develop their skills during the *debriefing*.

During the briefing part of the lesson and immediately prior to the group-work activity:

- Emphasise to pupils that the practical activity is a chance to *practise* the particular skills.
- Spend time talking with pupils not just about what they should be doing but also about *how* they can do it in practice.
- Get pupils to *anticipate* what problems may arise and how they should deal with them when they arise: for example, how they will deal with conflict.
- Emphasise to pupils *behaviour that you are looking for* during the group work (write this on the board), remind them during the group work and then follow this up at the end.

- *Model the behaviour* either directly or by participating in the activity with a pupil.
- *Reinforce* and highlight some of the group-work skills when using group or paired work in the curriculum.

During the group-work activity:

- Stop pupils during the activity to remind them of the objective or the skill they should be practising/thinking about ('What I'm looking for' – WILF – is described in Part II, p. 98).

During the debriefing part of the lesson, encourage pupils to:

- *Reflect* on their behaviour and group interaction so that they can do it better in the future.
- *Evaluate* how well they performed the particular skill(s).

Following these guidelines will help to raise pupils' awareness of the skills they are supposed to be practising, but more importantly it will give them ideas and ways in which they can put their skills into practice and indicate how they can adapt and develop those skills.

Some group members do not get involved in the group work

All group members are supposed to contribute to the group, but there may be a number of reasons why pupils do not get involved in the group work. They may be free riding, they may be shy, they may have personal reasons for not engaging with others, or they may be discouraged from involvement.

Free riders: leaving the work to others

We can get around this problem by:

- Making greater use of small groups (up to four) and paired work unless the groups can be broken down into sub-groups to do different aspects of a task (e.g. see Structuring the group-work activity, p. 48).
- Using 'snowballing' – where individual or paired work feeds into small group work, formed by combining pairs. Using individual work to feed into larger groupings can ensure that everyone has done at least some work in preparation for the group work.
- Allocating roles to group members each time a piece of group work is started so that particular children are not always able to opt for the easiest role (e.g. timekeeper) and are given opportunities to develop their group-work skills.
- Making individuals accountable to the group. You could evaluate individuals on their contributions to the group work. Alternatively, you could base the group assessment on the sum of individual assessments (or the lowest-scoring

member provides the score for the whole group) or group members' contribution to the group work. You could also structure the task so that group members are interdependent by allowing only particular members access to essential information or knowledge required by the group to complete their task.

Shy children

- Shy children may find it easier to contribute in pairs, and more so with friends. Try to make sure that if they are in a small group they are with at least one friend. Build up groups with shy children much more carefully from pairs to threes and then fours.
- Stable groups breed familiarity between pupils in terms of procedures, trust and positive conflict and are thus good for encouraging shy pupils.
- Encourage shy children to participate and give them positive feedback. Part of the reason for their shyness may be a lack of confidence.
- Do not discourage them by pushing them into high risk roles (e.g. spokesperson) too early.
- If shy children are attentive and understand the work well it may be better to allow them to participate by just listening to the group discussion. As long as they are actively involved when work needs to be done then the rest of the group should not become frustrated with them.
- If, after repeated attempts, shy children remain unforthcoming, group them with other shy children or encourage them to take a bit of a risk with a chairing or spokesperson role.

Group members ignore or exclude non-participants

Sometimes it is easier to ignore those who do not contribute to the group work. However, this does not resolve the problem and may even reinforce it. Not listening to others' contributions, interrupting and talking over others can all have a debilitating effect on the group ethos.

- Sometimes pupils have natural difficulties speaking to more than one or two others and often talk simultaneously, interrupt or ignore others. Using smaller groupings can overcome this.
- Remind the group of how important it is for all of them to participate and encourage them to elicit contributions actively from those who do not participate.
- Assess the group or get the group members to evaluate themselves on their level of participation and listening. Alternatively, the teacher or a pupil observer could assess the group. When this becomes part of the group evaluation or outcome non-participants are more likely to be encouraged to join in.
- Group roles can be allocated by the teacher so that weaker pupils remain involved or dominant pupils do not take over.

- Have a quiet word with non-participants and encourage them to join in. Find out if there is a good reason for them not joining in. It may be that others have not appreciated their contributions in the past or that they have been ignored.
- Non-participation may be an indication that the group member is struggling with the task. (He or she may disagree with it or feel it is irrelevant).

To encourage listening to others:

- During briefing or debriefing, ask group members how they show they are listening and what it feels like when they are not listened to or are interrupted. Ask them to think about how they can help someone who does not listen to them.
- Introduce a task where group members note down the gist of what others have said. In the debriefing you could suggest that those who did not feel they did this very well could try harder to listen to others in future.
- Emphasise during briefing and the lesson that you are looking for evidence of listening to and involvement of others. This could be written on the board as 'What I am looking for' (WILF). You could pick up on those who are not listening. You could also explicitly evaluate group members on their listening and inclusive behaviour.

Groups split into smaller groupings

Groups may split into smaller groups for any number of reasons. This can be due to the use of large groups, materials that encourage individual working and pupils not being sufficiently close together.

- In large groups, pupils who are inexperienced in group work may have problems speaking and listening to all of the other children in the group. Smaller groupings can help overcome this. Think about reinforcing social and communication skills in these groups.
- Multiple pens and sheets of paper to write on or to read from often lead to a group splitting into smaller sub-groups/individuals or arguments about what colour pens to use and so on. The better tasks have tended to involve groups or pairs working with just one large piece of paper and a single pen.
- Too much space or obstacles between group members encourages groups to break into sub-groups or members to be edged out of the group. A group of four around a single rectangular table encourages pupils to work as a whole group. If more space is needed later for the practical activity then a second table (but no more) can be added. If the groups need more space then sitting on the floor can allow proximity and the space to do the work. Furniture removal takes up time and is demanding on the teacher. With consistency and practice, the time taken to do this can be reduced.
- Pupils should be encouraged to think about where they will sit in relation to each other so that they can see, speak, listen and interact with the rest of the group easily. Encourage face-to-face seating with at most two persons sitting in a row.

Low attaining and pupils with special educational needs do not participate in group work

This is a tricky problem since it might be that these children feel intimidated or pushed out by the more able students or they may be reluctant to get involved because of reduced confidence or an inability to see that their skills might contribute something of value. It is important to: (a) break down any resistances these children have to participating, (b) inspire confidence in their own abilities to contribute (and support others), and (c) encourage other group members to go out of their way to support and help these pupils.

- Emphasise the value of working with all types of people in the real world, that we all bring particular skills to the table.
- Ensure that during class briefing and debriefing the issue of how important it is to actively involve others and how to go about doing this is emphasised.
- Publicly acknowledge in front of other pupils in the class the special and particular skills that these children have and how they can contribute to group work. Reward these children for their efforts and others for supporting them.
- Provide these children a particular role that fits well with their skills and enables them to get involved and to contribute in a positive way to group working. Alternatively, put them in a position of responsibility so that peers have to involve them and treat them with respect.
- Consider 'skilling these children up' in some way (e.g. see the Jigsaw grouping section in Chapter 9) so that they have specific skills or knowledge that the rest of the class do not have and that they have something that only they can share.
- Get these children working as a tutor within a peer tutoring activity so that they get used to teaching others and develop the confidence in their own skills. Peer tutoring could be with less able children or younger children from other classes.
- It may be helpful for the group to receive some coaching (see Chapter 7) in the form of encouragement of positive attitudes and positive ways to include all group members or particular children.
- In some cases the child with SEN may need some constructive support and advice to help them integrate into the group-work activity.

It may be helpful for the group to receive some supportive coaching (see Chapter 7) in the form of encouragement of positive attitudes and positive ways to include and involve the child with SEN. In some cases, the child with SEN may need some constructive support and advice to help him or her integrate into the group-work activity. These might be part of briefing or debriefing (see Chapter 5).

The group is unable to handle conflict, make decisions or reach a compromise or consensus

Pupils often find it difficult to make joint decisions or resolve conflict. Conflict is quite normal in group work and actually is a main impetus in the success of group working. It is also a central stage in a group's development - unless particular issues are resolved, the group is unable to perform to the best of its ability. It is important, however, to avoid petty disputes that are unresolvable.

Conflict about ideas that are central to the task can be advantageous as long as members are encouraged to explore each other's reasoning with a view to coming to a compromise or consensus. Sometimes people have to agree to disagree and the teacher should explain that it is not a bad thing to hold different views. However, this should not be used as an excuse to prevent group members from debating the issue in the first place. You and your pupils should not allow conflict to destroy the group.

- Conflict is a major difficulty that children face, and thus they may benefit from class discussion of specific instances to resolve or learn from them.
- Clear ways of dealing with conflict may need to be agreed upon and incorporated into the ground rules for group working.
- Get pupils to anticipate what problems might arise and how they will deal with them: for example, how to deal with conflict, what to do to come to a consensus and so on.
- Encourage pupils to think about how a compromise could be reached.
- Make it part of the chair's role to mediate, have the last word, suggest a compromise and so on.
- Establish ownership of the conflict. Which members of the group feel the conflict and are being affected by it? Include those members of the group who are not directly involved in the conflict. How does the conflict make them feel? Also distinguish between people, actions and opinions so that actions that cause conflict are resolved and differences of opinion are discussed.
- It might be useful for children to write down their thoughts about the conflict. This gives them time to think through the conflict when alone and away from an emotionally charged situation.
- Allow pupils an opportunity to have time out so that they can escape from the conflict. Allowing this means that they do not feel trapped and are more likely to try to resolve the conflict. As a last resort, allow them to change groups. However, individual pupils should not be allowed to do this too often as they will gain a reputation as a troublemaker.
- Consider repeating some trust and communication activities with the group/class.

Group members disrupt the group or class

This can be a tough nut to crack. Though it takes less courage to be disruptive in small group situations than in class settings, teachers should not consider resorting to whole class instruction. Disruption in a group is often restricted to a very small proportion of the class, thus allowing the remainder to get on undisrupted. On some occasions there may be no easy solution other than restructuring the groups.

- First make sure that it really is disruption. It might simply be a healthy, if heated, group discussion.

- It may be useful to ask yourself whether the disruption is aimed at others within the group, others in another group or even at the teacher. Quite often, disruptive behaviour can be for the teacher's benefit.
- The disruptive behaviour may be a symptom of a dysfunctional group: for example, if one sex is dominating the group task (girls are as culpable as boys), group members mistrust each other and so on. It is thus important to find out why group members are being disruptive.
- Try to encourage the disruptive child's contribution to the group by focusing on their positive contributions.
- You could have a chat with the disruptive child and see if they have any reasons for being disruptive. Ask them what would help them not to be so disruptive.
- Ensure that tasks have clear and definable goals.
- Friendship groups may result in disruption, especially if the class does not have a positive view of group work or if the task is insufficiently challenging.
- Where general disruption has occurred within a group, ask pupils to discuss during debriefing how to overcome disruption next time.

Group members do not do their jobs

This can be a particular problem, especially when pupils are given roles that come into play only for a short period of the task, for example, spokesperson or timekeeper.

- Structuring the task with short deadlines may keep group members on their toes. Remind the group that their deadline is approaching or that they should be starting a particular aspect of the task.
- It may be useful to have the task instructions written on the board or on sheets of paper to ensure that pupils know what they are to do.
- You could also try to ensure that the first part of the task is short and simple so that all are engaged from the start. If the group has to start by making complex decisions from the word go, this can be a licence for some to let others get on with it.

Solutions specific to group-work roles

Some pupils get caught between performing their role and being a group member, resulting in acting out just one role or doing a bad job of both. Other children are unsure how to perform their role in practice.

- Ensure that group members know what is involved in their roles and how the role can be put into practice. This is better written down, maybe as a job description. Emphasise that roles are in addition to being an active group member. This could be a feature of group rules.
- Allocate roles to pupils rather than allowing them to choose their own (at least at first) so that the complexity of the role is matched to the ability of the child.
- Encourage pupils to see their role as a group member as more important than their specialised role.
- Only use roles when really necessary.

Group work starts off well but then fades

This can happen when too much time is allowed for group work, when groups have had a break or when the main aim of the activity has been completed.

- Keep the group busy. Consider giving short deadlines and or giving the group too much work to complete in a given time period (although you will have to allow time for finishing at a later point). Use this strategy with care, since pupils get annoyed when they are not given enough time to complete their work.
- Make the final stage of group work important for learners. This can be where they are assessed, or where they think about the lessons they have learned from group work.
- Get the group to summarise what they have done at the end and make this an integral part of the task: for example, to give feedback to the rest of the class.

A member dominates the group or is over-talkative

Dominant characters can be a particular problem, especially when they want to do everything. They may be well intentioned but they need to be discouraged from dominating the group. This can be handled in a number of ways:

- Have a class discussion on the pros and cons of dominant group members. Get pupils to reflect on how dominant they are and to talk about when they feel they have been too dominant or not sufficiently dominant.
- Have a quiet word with the dominant pupil. Emphasise your pleasure that he or she is so keen to contribute but encourage him or her to let others contribute, too and take more of a lead role. Suggest that dominant pupils say only some of the things that they think so that they avoid trying to fill every silence. They could also encourage others to speak up.
- Allocate roles to the group and give the dominant member a less centrally involved role or maybe even encourage him or her to observe the group or another group containing a dominant child.
- Have a discussion with the group encouraging them to reflect on how they are functioning. Ask them various questions about how well the group is working and then slip in questions about who said the most, whether someone spoke too much, whether someone took the lead, whether there was anything they thought but did not say, why they did not say this, and so on.
- Remove the person from the group and put him or her in a group where members are more assertive in speaking up.

Some members act like know-it-alls

The group ethos and ability to get the work done can be restricted by know-it-alls. Some of the suggestions for dominant group members can be applied to this problem. Also:

- You could allow the group to sort out the know-it-all themselves. The group will be keen to tell the know-it-all when they are proved wrong. It may be prudent to step in at this point and have a word with the person showing the know-all behaviour. If you do not intervene, the group ethos may deteriorate.

The group is very passive

Sometimes groups can be very passive and avoid making decisions or having discussions. They are often extremely dependent on the teacher. This usually occurs when group work is first introduced. Pupils will feel insecure and unsure what they are to do, and may be concerned about getting the 'right' answer.

- You need to allay their fears. Avoid being too directive or critical. Tell them that there are no right or wrong answers (though some answers may be better than others).
- Encourage groups to find out things for themselves. Where could they look to find the piece of information they need?
- Allow groups to discover things for themselves and to learn from their mistakes.
- Avoid changing the group's ideas – pupils can feel very dejected when an adult changes their ideas or actively rejects them. At most, suggest a variety of ideas.
- If the group is uncritical of ideas (i.e. they accept ideas without discussion), the teacher could try to introduce some conflict by questioning whether anyone disagrees with the view or can challenge the consensus.

The group does not engage in discussion

Pupils often do not engage in much discussion but rather get on with the practical activity of writing. This may be because they feel a pressure to produce the work or to appear as though they are getting on and achieving something.

- Explicitly set time aside for group discussion before starting the practical work.
- Withhold materials for the practical side of the task until the groups have finished their discussion or for a set amount of time.
- Avoid the practical side of the task altogether if it really is unnecessary.
- Structure the discussion with some specific questions to make it clear what you want the pupils to discuss and how to go about doing it.
- It may be helpful to review the role of exploratory talk in your class. Neil Mercer's Talk programme (Dawes et al., 2000 in Useful references and resources on p. 99) may be helpful.

The group spends too much time talking off task

Group-work situations are most beneficial when the talk is on task and members learn from each other by explaining things to one another. One of the major benefits of group learning is its informal nature, as long as social chatter does not prevent the group from achieving its aims. There are various ways to deal with off-task talk:

- Check that social chat really is a problem. You may find that it is infrequent and sometimes it forms part of an explanation between group members.
- Your proximity to the group should reduce the amount of social chat, so make more frequent visits to the vicinity of the group.
- If off-task chatter becomes a serious problem and is not just restricted to isolated occasions, you could consider discussing this with the group and bringing up the problem in debriefing.

Some group members criticise others

A negative group ethos is a significant contributory factor in the failure of group work. Putting others down for their ideas or inability to do particular tasks is a main cause of a negative group ethos. When pupils are so used to having to compete with other children in the class for rewards and praise, it may be difficult to break out of a cycle of derogatory comments between them. There also can be a fine line between positive, constructive feedback and regular negative (though maybe similarly constructive) feedback.

- Discourage pupils from dismissing the ideas of other group members. Encourage pupils to find something positive to say about each other's ideas.
- Have a discussion about maintaining a positive group atmosphere where pupils think about how they felt when others put them or their ideas down. Raise the issues of anger, frustration, revenge, low self-confidence and similar feelings and ask what effects they may have on group working.
- Encourage children to watch their language (avoid negative language like 'poor', 'bad', 'unsatisfactory') and body language (sighs, grimaces) which may cause problems by hurting other people's feelings.
- Step back and repeat some trust and communication activities.

Gender issues are disrupting the group

Gender issues can arise during group work. The easiest way to avoid these problems is to take the necessary steps in the first place (see Group composition, p. 31):

- Balance the sexes within a group. If this is impossible then ensure that where a child of one sex is in a minority that they either get on with the other children in the group or are sufficiently strong in character to stand up for him- or herself and not feel isolated.
- One sex may often talk off task while the other does the work. If possible, have two boys and two girls on a rectangular desk, with girls facing each other diagonally across the desk.
- Try to prevent boys from taking charge of the equipment (computers, science or sport apparatus).
- Avoid encouraging competition between the sexes or siding with one or the other (if this ever happens).

Group work is disorganised

If groups are poor at organising their group work, then they will not be able to achieve the task very well. This is particularly a problem in creative tasks, when pupils are keen to get on with the doing of the activity.

- Scaffold the groups' planning and organising of the task. Initially you may wish to structure the task yourself and set short deadlines, regular reports back to the class, and repeated reminders of the timing of the activity (i.e. what they should be starting or finishing at that point). Ask pupils to think together about how they will approach the task during the briefing phase of the lesson. Encourage them to devise a plan of action.
- Once pupils are better at thinking about how they will do the task, allocate time at the start of the group work where pupils are expected to plan what they will do and how they will do it.

Pupils' group-work skills are not improving

There may be a number of reasons why pupils' group-work skills do not improve. Think about whether the problem is that they are not applying and practising what they see as good group-work skills or whether they are just not building on their skills.

- Look at the suggestions in Group members do not practise what they preach, above (p. 81).
- Ask pupils how their specific skills are developing. Get them to self-evaluate after group work and encourage them to think about how they can improve their skills in the future. Remind them of this immediately prior to future group work.
- Repeat earlier trust and communication activities.

Motivating pupils

Some children just will not do group work. These children may be uncompromising and disruptive in the group, or may try to free ride or attempt to work independently. They need to learn that group work can be fun and that they have more to gain from doing it. This might mean creating extrinsic rewards (e.g. merits, stars, competition rewards, marbles/tokens) to draw them in, in the hope that intrinsic rewards will then take over.

- Give greater value to the group product and encourage taking part in group work, for example by giving the whole group an extrinsic reward when the child is involved and has worked well with others.
- Introduce some sense of competition or evaluation of the products. Each of the other groups or individuals could award points (discreetly) under different

criteria for each group output (never their own). Then the points could be added up to find a winner, but not a loser.

- Allow the child to opt out, but encourage him or her to take on an observer role so that he or she can look for good group work, communication and so on.
- Move the awkward child to a successful group that is stable and mature enough to cope with him or her and value his or her contributions, especially when he or she has to compromise, etc. This is risky, but after a few attempts things may settle.
- Encourage the child to take a risk – by compromising, or being quiet, or not being argumentative or fussy.

Teaching Assistants or other adults dominate group interactions

One of the hardest things for teachers and particularly Teaching Assistants (TAs) to do is to avoid intervening in group work too early. From an adult's perspective it can be easy to see where groups are going wrong and to want to put them right or to give them advice on how to do something better or more quickly. The temptation to intervene can be much greater when time is short or when this is part of the adult's role in the classroom (e.g. to support or instruct an individual or small group). Even relatively short interventions can involve the adult dominating the activity and being overly didactic. However, such interventions do not allow children to learn from their own mistakes or to take ownership of their group work and their learning. Similarly it is all too easy to focus on the outcome of the task rather than the process (which is often the more important part of the activity) and the reasoning and decision making that got the group there. Some useful ways to improve the way adults engage with groups are as follows:

- It is important to ensure that the teacher, TAs and any other adults are aware of the ideas presented in Chapter 7 on how and when to intervene and work with groups as well as with the main ideas presented in this first section of the handbook.
- Encourage TAs and other adults to avoid intervening in group work too early. If and when they do intervene they should also avoid dominating or directing the interactions within the group and try to preserve the dialogue between members of the group. Asking questions that help group members get their collaborative work back on track can be one useful way of doing this.
- Encourage the TA or other adult to monitor and listen in to the group's interaction without intervening at all. The adult might be asked to circulate around the classroom looking for examples of positive group interaction which can then be reported back and discussed as a class at the end of the session.
- For situations when the TA or adult intervenes in group work, encourage him or her to only use open-ended questions (ones requiring more than a 'yes' or 'no' response) and to avoid answering the questions for the children him- or herself. If pupils are unsure what is meant by the question or about how to respond, then the adult should clarify or rephrase the question. This questioning could

also focus on promoting pupils' thinking about the task and the group interaction rather than the completion of the task and the outcome.

- The teacher could view working with TAs and other adults in the classroom as a form of professional development or coaching. As part of this, teachers and/ or facilitators might use briefing and debriefing to support the TAs in their classroom in developing their own skills in supporting and facilitating groups, thinking each time about what did or did not go well. They should also think about how they could improve the way they work with and support groups next time. It would be useful to return to these points before subsequent sessions involving pupil group working to boost development in these skills.

I work in a very traditional school/society, and other staff and parents are questioning whether group work can be effective in these circumstances

From experience of many studies of group work in a number of countries around the world, we have found that our approach has contributed to learning and social enhancement of pupils in 'traditional' and 'child-centred' societies. In traditional societies where neither other teachers nor parents have previously encountered the benefits of effective group work, there may be resistance to this different approach within the classroom. Things you can do to persuade these people are to:

- Ensure that you brief and debrief your class to allow all students ownership of group working in the classroom.
- Ensure that the early activities are fun and interesting; having the pupils on your side is half of the battle.
- Introduce group-work activities more gently and possibly in parts of the curriculum where they are more likely to be accepted (e.g. during physical education, drama, science, English and so on).
- It may be helpful to write a letter to parents explaining this innovative approach and citing that in controlled studies we have consistently found this approach to group working has brought learning and social benefits to all children in the class. It may be worthwhile adding that high attainers benefit as well as low- and mid-attainers.
- In many traditional societies, children will work collectively on their homework outside of the classroom. The implementation of group working within the classroom draws upon these informal skills – legitimising enhanced sharing for learning within the classroom.
- It would be helpful to ask another teacher in your school to implement the same group-working programme. With the support of a colleague, you will have someone to share your thoughts about benefits and concerns of group work. Further, you will have a valuable ally in your school in case anyone questions why your pedagogic approach is different from most other teachers in the school. It may even help matters if your school took on a whole school plan for group work.

Further information

There is much research out there and there are many different approaches to encouraging children to work together. In addition to the extended list of articles and chapters arising from the original SPRinG project (see Chapter 1), below are books and articles that provide further discussion about, and alternative approaches to, group work.

Barron, B. (2003). 'When smart groups fail.' *The Journal of the Learning Sciences*, 12(3), 307-395.

Cohen, E. (1994). *Designing Groupwork: Strategies for the Heterogeneous Classroom* (2nd Edition). New York: Teachers College Press.

Cohen, E. (1994). 'Restructuring the classroom: Conditions for productive small groups.' *Review of Educational Research*, 64(1), 1-35.

Cowie, H. & Rudduck, J. (1988). *Learning Together: Working Together*. London: BP Educational Services.

Dunne, E. & Bennett, N. (1990). *Talking and Learning in Groups*. London and Basingstoke: Macmillan Education.

Fountain, S. (1990). *Learning Together: Global Education*. Cheltenham: Stanley Thornes.

Gillies, R. (2016). 'Cooperative learning: Review of research and practice.' *Australian Journal of Teacher Education*, 41(3), 39-54.

Gillies, R. M. (2007). *Cooperative Learning: Integrating Theory and Practice*. London: Sage.

Hall, E., Hall, C. & Leech, A. (1990). *Scripted Fantasy in the Classroom*. London: Routledge.

Howe, C. (2010). *Peer groups and children's development: Psychological and educational perspectives*. Oxford: Wiley-Blackwell.

Johnson, D. & Johnson, F. (2013). *Joining Together: Group Theory and Group Skills* (11th Edition). London: Pearson.

Jolliffe, W. (2007). *Cooperative Learning in the Classroom: Putting it into Practice*. Sage.

Kagan, S. & Kagan, M. (2009). *Kagan Cooperative Learning*. San Clemente, CA: Kagan.

Kutnick, P. & Rogers, C. (1994). *Groups in Schools*. London: Cassell.

Mercer, N. (2000). *Words and Minds: How We Use Language to Think Together*. London: Routledge.

Mercer, N., Wegerif, R., & Dawes, L. (1999). 'Children's talk and the development of reasoning in the classroom.' *British Educational Research Journal*, 25(1), 95-111.

Slavin, R. (2001). *A Practical Guide to Cooperative Learning*. Boston: Allyn & Bacon.

Topping, K. (2005). 'Trends in peer learning.' *Educational Psychology*, 25(6), 631-645.

Tuckman, B. (1965). 'Developmental sequence in small groups'. *Psychological Bulletin*, 63, 384-99.

Webb, N. M. (2009). 'The teacher's role in promoting collaborative dialogue in the classroom'. *British Journal of Educational Psychology*, 79, 1-28.

Webb, N. M. & Palincsar, A. S. (1996). 'Group processes in the classroom'. In D. C. Berliner & R. C. Calfee (Eds.), *Handbook of Educational Psychology* (pp. 841-73). New York: Macmillan.

Part II

Group work and training activities for your class

Introduction

Children's progress at school will be affected by the quality of relationships in class and their positive attitude. These can be aided by teachers ensuring that experiences help children develop a positive sense of themselves and constructive relationships with others. This section outlines a relational approach based on a number of social, communication and advanced group-work skills activities. The activities have been ordered into a developmental progression of complexity, with certain activities building on others (as explained in Chapter 5). We suggest that your class undertakes two or three activities per week at the start of the school year, progressing from initial social skills (trust, sensitivity) through communication and advanced group-working skills that can (eventually) be integrated into curriculum-based tasks. Remember that the activities are progressive; thus, it is often worthwhile repeating some of the earlier activities when/if your pupils' group working becomes tentative or ineffective. Also, note that this is an indicative listing. You can develop the activities by adjusting the content or duration, or by extending the ideas and group work into other areas of the curricula. You can also develop and use your own activities and may find many other sources for further group working (see references below for some suggestions).

Age suitability

As described in Chapter 9, we have divided age-appropriate activities into **lower primary**, **upper primary** and **primary** to cover age groups 4 to 7 years, 8 to 11 years and 4 to 11 years, respectively. You will notice a heading at the start of each section indicating the recommended age range for the activity. However, this age range is only a rough estimate to give you a quick guide: you will find that some younger children are capable of undertaking an 'older' activity, and older children may enjoy a 'younger' activity.

Stable groups

You will notice that many of the tasks refer to the use of stable groups (see Chapter 4). You should use these activities to help determine the groups that you plan to use. It is quite important that children do the activities in the groups that they will be in for a substantial period of time. The activities are about building up relationships, trust, respect and so on between group members to help them work better together; this will not happen if the groups are frequently changed.

'What I'm looking for'–WILF

One difficulty that you may encounter when working through the activities is that pupils are very good at saying what they should do but are poor at putting it into practice. The trick is to connect the group-work activity explicitly to the briefing discussion beforehand, since these activities are 'opportunities' for pupils to try out their skills. Teachers can also encourage the practical use of communication skills by ensuring pupils use ground rules for group talk and by emphasising the skills that the teacher is looking for (we use the heading 'What I'm looking for' - WILF). In this way you can note (on the board or elsewhere) what skills and behaviour you would like to see when pupils are interacting, and you can remind them of these during the group-work activities.

Safety and security of your pupils

As we have stressed throughout this handbook, children need to develop their group-working skills from a basis of trust, security and sensitivity. It is important that the classroom environment (or wherever your class undertakes these activities) also provides a place of safety and security. Each activity asks children to become involved either physically or psychologically. For children to engage fully in these activities, it is best to arrange the environment so that there is:

- little likelihood that a child will stumble over an obstacle;
- enough room for all children to move around without bumping into each other; and
- enough equipment for all children to participate at the same time (or in a particular order).

You must check your school's health and safety policy for guidelines. As the teacher, you should consider how well the children are briefed, so that they understand and are able to undertake the activity. You should also keep a sharp lookout for any potential conflict (as discussed in Chapter 11) and any possibility of an accident taking place. Once your class begins to develop and become more confident in their group-working skills, many of these safety and security issues will be resolved as second nature. And, as you and your class become more competent in using the skills, everyone will enjoy engaging in these activities. *If you are in any doubt about the suitability of a session or activity for your pupils, do not use it.*

Below, we suggest a range of activity sessions, but first there are some important points to note:

- Sessions can be used flexibly - from thirty minutes to over an hour in length.
- Timings are approximate and can be extended or reduced as appropriate.

- The activity sequence is developmental and thus group-work activities should not be used selectively or in different sections (although you can always draw upon/repeat previous activities).
- In most cases the expectation is that the groups used are the *stable groups* you set up towards the start of the term.
- It is essential that you allow time for *briefing* and *debriefing*, as these are the times when pupils are thinking and learning about how to develop their skills.
- The *teacher information sheets* are designed to help you carry out the lesson and group activities.
- There are also *worksheets* for pupils which you can photocopy.

Useful references and resources

There are many other resource books that can provide further activities for developing sensitivity, awareness, trust and respect or communication skills and advanced group skills. These need to be considered carefully to ensure that they do actually encourage the desired skills or behaviours. Sometimes these activities may require adjustment and some trial and error to be appropriate for group work skills training. Be creative and have fun with whatever you try. We have found that books that outline activities for youth groups, sports training and for children's parties can sometimes be useful especially for team building, social skills training and for fun, though may be less useful for developing specific communication skills or advanced group working skills. Other resources are available from the SPRinG project website (www.spring-project.org.uk).

Curry, M. & Bromfield, C. (1998). *Circle Time In-service Training Manual*. Tamworth: NASEN.
Dawes, L., Mercer, N. & Wegerif, R. (2000). *Thinking Together: A Programme of Lessons and Activities*. Birmingham: Questions.
Dearling, A., Armstrong, H. & Neville, J. (1994). *The New Youth Games Book*. Dorset: Russell House.
Farivar, S. & Webb, N. (1991). *Helping Behavior Activities Handbook: Cooperative Small Group Problem Solving in Middle School Mathematics*. Los Angeles: UCLA.
Fraser, K., Fraser, L. & Fraser, M. (2009). *The 175 Best Camp Games: A Handbook for Leaders*. Ontario, Canada: Boston Mills Press.
Leech, N. & Wooster, A. D. (1986). *Personal and Social Skills: A Practical Approach for the Classroom*. Exeter: Religious and Moral Education Press.
Race, P. (2000). *500 Tips on Group Learning*. London: Kogan Page.
Stanford, G. (1990). *Developing Effective Classroom Groups*. Bristol: Acora Books.
Thacker, J., Stoate, P. & Feest, G. (1992). *Using Group Work in the Primary Classroom*. Crediton: Southgate.

Group work and group-work rules

PRIMARY

Resources

Distribute 1 pen and paper per group.

Learning objectives

- To think about working with others
- To develop rules for working with others in pairs and groups

Briefing (15–20 minutes)

Hold a class discussion about working with others in pairs and groups. This is your chance to find out what children think about working together and what their expectations are.

Explain to pupils that this year they will be working together a lot, maybe more than they have before. Find out what they think about working together.

- Do they enjoy it?
- Do they think they work better when working with others?
- Do they think they learn more?
- Do they prefer working with a partner or in groups?
- What sorts of people (discourage identification of others by name) do they think they work with best: friends, more able, less able, same ability, girls, boys, etc.?
- How can they expand their work choices?

Explain that in order for groups and pairs to work well together, they will need to decide on some ground rules for their group work.

Group work (10–15 minutes)

Ask groups (of two to four) to brainstorm ten rules for group working. They should note these on a large piece of rough paper. Give them five minutes for this. They then should spend the next five to ten minutes choosing what they believe to be the four most important rules.

Class work (10–15 minutes)

Have each group report the four important rules they chose and write them on the board to form a class list. As a whole class, try to reduce the list down to five main rules. The resulting rules should be incorporated as guides for class behaviour and displayed around the classroom. Good examples of rules might draw on the following:

- Involve everybody and encourage others to speak up.
- Trust and cooperate with each other.
- Respect each other's views and ideas.
- Take turns to speak, don't interrupt.
- Listen actively.
- Help and support each other.
- Suggest and share ideas and information.
- Support ideas with reasons.
- Think of alternative ideas and reasons.
- Be prepared to change your view.
- Take responsibility for your group and the work.
- Be positive about working together.

Debriefing (10 minutes)

Ask groups how they got on in their group work. What was positive about working together? What did not go so well? What would they try to improve next time and how will they go about doing that?

Follow-up work

Try reviewing the rules for working together later in the term as ideas will move on once the children have had a chance to get used to group work.

Unit 2

Sensitivity and awareness

PRIMARY

Below are five activities for developing sensitivity and awareness of others. These can be used separately with briefing and debriefing to form a thirty-minute session or in combination to form longer sessions.

Resources

Tasks 2.1–2.4 require space such as that in a gym or hall. Task 2.2 requires pieces of string or chalked lines long enough for at least eight people to stand on. Task 2.3 requires one or more large gym mats or something similar to act as a turtle shell.

Learning objectives

- To develop an understanding of trust, openness and sensitivity to others
- To have fun with other members of their group and class

Task 2.1 – Mirror, mirror

Time: Two to three minutes for each pairing. Rotate children so that each child has worked with three or four different partners from their group by the end.
Group size: Create pairs from stable groups.

Briefing: How can you make sure you cooperate with each other in this task? It is best to begin with something simple and then progress to more difficult actions. Try not to explain what you are doing – just act it out and wait for your partner to mirror it.

Task: Pairs of children stand facing each other, approximately half a metre apart. One child should be designated as the actor; the other is supposed to be their mirror image. Give the children some 'scripts' to follow (see below), where they act out everyday activities. Tell the actor that they can do or say anything but that their partner can only follow their actions (since mirrors do not speak, etc.). The roles can then be reversed, with another 'script'. Possible scripts:

- Waking and getting up in the morning
- Getting ready for school
- Sitting and working in class
- Playing basketball/netball in slow motion

Debriefing: What did you find easy/difficult? Did you get better at copying as you worked together or was it more difficult as the expressions and actions became increasingly complicated? Were the actions harder to copy with a new partner? How well did you cooperate with each other?

Task 2.2 – Crossing the river

Time: Minimum of ten minutes for groups of eight; longer if a larger group.

Group size: Begin with groups of eight (combine stable groups) and extend gradually to the whole class.

Briefing: The whole group must work together to solve the problem. What are you going to have to think and plan before making your first move? What will aid cooperation?

Task: A piece of string or a line drawn with chalk is made to represent a bridge. Pupils are asked to line up along it. The teacher tells the group that the bridge spans a river full of crocodiles and piranha. The group task is to line up alphabetically, without letting anyone fall into the river. They must always have at least one foot on the bridge. Maybe put an 'obstacle' on the bridge so that swapping places becomes more difficult.

Debriefing: How did you help each other to line up? At what point in the task was cooperation most difficult? At what point in the task did cooperation become easier? What have you learned from this exercise?

Task 2.3 – Big turtle

Time: Ten minutes.

Group size: Begin with stable groups (fours) and gradually extend by adding members from another stable group.

Briefing: As for Task 2.2.

Task: A group of between four and eight pupils (wearing suitable clothes) get on their hands and knees under a large 'turtle shell' and try to move across the room. A gym mat works well as a shell but other materials – such as cardboard, a sheet, etc. – may be used. You could set up a course for the turtle to try to maneuvre around without losing its shell.

Debriefing: As for Task 2.2.

Task 2.4 – Group breathing

Time: Ten minutes.

Group size: Start with pairs (from stable groups) and then gradually increase in size to involve the whole class in one big circle, depending on the space available.

Briefing questions: What are you going to listen for? How will you know whether your neighbours are inhaling or exhaling? What strategies could you use to help synchronise your breathing (e.g. breathing faster or slower)?

Task: The group lies on the floor, face up in a circle, with their heads in the centre and their bodies radiating out. All members of the group hold hands and shut their eyes. The exercise is to try to breathe in and out at the same time as their neighbour and therefore with all the other members of their group. When this has been achieved the teacher asks the group to breathe in deeply together and then let out their breath slowly together, again doing this in synchronisation.

Debriefing questions: How easy was it to synchronise your normal breathing with one neighbour/two neighbours? What helped? What hindered? Did you get better at it as time went by?

Task 2.5 – I was frightened when...

Time: About twenty minutes.

Group size: Pairs (from stable groups - to combine back into stable groups).

Briefing: There might be things that some children cannot talk about. Suggest that they may like to talk about something else that is less frightening. How will you respond if the frightening thing is not frightening to you? Talk about what it means to trust someone.

Task: Carefully pair up children. Children take it in turns to finish the sentence 'I was frightened when...' Issues that arise are discussed between paired children. Pairs reverse the order of who goes first and exchange sentences of 'I was happy when...' If appropriate, pairs join with another pair to form their stable group and continue the exchange.

Debriefing questions: Was it easier or harder to speak about being happy? As the listener, what skills did you need to use? Are there any other emotions you would be prepared to share with your peers?

Unit 3

Developing trust

PRIMARY

Following are five activities to develop trust and cooperation between group members.

Resources

All tasks require space such as that in a gym or hall.

Learning objectives

- To develop a sense of trust and cooperation in a group
- To have fun with other members of the group and class

Task 3.1 – Trust train

Time: Ten minutes.

Group size: Start in pairs from stable groups and build up, but do not allow the train to become too large and unwieldy.

Briefing: What potential problems might arise in this activity? How can we avoid them? Drivers must not direct the group into potential danger. Everyone (except the driver) must abide by the rule of keeping their eyes shut, and everyone (including the driver) must not run or do anything else that may hurt or harm another. Signals need to be clear and timed ahead. Everyone has a responsibility to pass the signal quickly and accurately. If collisions occur, no one should be blamed.

Task: Pairs stand one behind the other. The child at the back (the driver, with eyes open) rests their hands on the shoulders of the child in front, who has their eyes shut. The driver signals how the train is to move by pressing on the shoulders of the child in front. A press on the left shoulder signals the train is to turn left. A press on the right shoulder signals the train is to turn right. A gentle pull with both hands signals stop. And a gentle press forward means forward. When you add more children to the train, the signals are transmitted down the train from the child at the back to the next child in line. Make journeys around the room, ensuring that the trains do not bump into each other. Change the driver and repeat the exercise until everyone has had a turn as the driver. You could add a course to maneuvre around for extra fun.

Debriefing questions: Was it easier to be the driver or part of the train? What made it easy or difficult to work together? Did each driver anticipate the direction and speed needed to take the train on a safe journey? What group size was the most manageable? What did you feel about others who did not cooperate? If it was felt that drivers deliberately directed the group into danger, what effect did this have on the trust between group members?

Task 3.2 – Face trust

Time: Ten minutes.

Group size: Pairs of children from their stable groups.

Briefing: What does it mean to trust someone? How can someone lose your trust? How important is it to trust other people in the group/class?

Task: Only use this task if you know that children will behave responsibly, with due attention to health and safety, and check your school's health and safety policy for guidelines on physical contact. Pairs of children stand face to face with their eyes closed. They gently feel their partner's face, hair and neck with their fingertips. You should emphasise that this is best done as quietly and as gently as possible. One variation is that half the children remain with their eyes closed while you provide them with a new partner. Pupils then have to guess through touch alone who that new partner is. You might want to limit the number of pairs doing this at one time to ensure that children act responsibly (e.g. three pairs, with the rest of the class as an audience).

Debriefing questions: How did this exercise make you feel? How easy was it to do the activity? Were you embarrassed? How important is it that we take responsibility for the safety of other people whom we work with?

Task 3.3 – Arches

Time: Ten minutes.

Group size: Pairs of children from their stable groups.

Briefing: As for Task 3.2.

Task: Only use this task if you know that children will behave responsibly, with due attention to health and safety, and check your school's health and safety policy for guidelines. Pairs of children stand facing each other. They hold their arms out straight in front of them and move forward until their fingertips just touch. They should gradually lean forward until their palms are touching and try to find a balance point between partners. If they go too far then they will fall forward. Emphasise to pupils that they should *on no account* allow another person to fall forward. If there are any concerns that this may happen then this activity should not be used. Repeat the activity with another member from their stable group.

Debriefing questions: As for Task 3.2. Also: were you worried that your partner may let you fall?

Task 3.4 – Leaning out

Time: Ten minutes.

Group size: Pairs of children from their stable groups.

Briefing and debriefing: As for Task 3.3.

Task: Only use this task if you know that children will behave responsibly, with due attention to health and safety, and check your school's health and safety policy for guidelines. Pairs of children stand facing each other with their feet touching toe to toe. Pupils link hands or use a safety grip (each person holds on to the wrists of the other - the other person cannot then let go). Children then lean backwards and try to find the balance point. If the balance point is lost then they will begin to fall backwards. Repeat the activity with another member from their stable group.

Task 3.5 – Cooperative letters and shapes

Time: Ten minutes.

Group size: Pairs or fours from their stable groups.

Briefing and debriefing: As for Task 3.3.

Task: Forming letters and shapes may seem simple, but working with a partner requires each child to help and support the other. Groups are asked to form a simple letter, like an 'L' or an 'O'. Progressively the shapes become more complex - 'S', 'M' and 'R'. You can also use simple and complex shapes, from a circle to a parallelogram to a pentagon.

Sensitivity, respect and sharing views

PRIMARY

Provided are three activities to develop sensitivity, respect and positivity in the class.

Resources

Photocopy Worksheet 4a for Task 4.1 and Worksheet 4b for Task 4.2. One sheet per group is needed. Cut up sheets into individual cards.

Learning objectives

- To enhance self-awareness and sensitivity to others' thoughts and feelings
- To encourage openness, cooperation and the sharing of views between children

Task 4.1 – Truth game

Time: Twenty minutes.

Group size: Children should work in their stable groups (fours).

Briefing questions: How will you make sure everyone has a go at answering a question? How should you react if someone says something that you do not agree with or you dislike?

Task: Each group places the cards from Worksheet 4a face down in the middle of the group. Explain to the groups that members take it in turns to select a card and try to answer the question as truthfully as possible. Other group members should find out why the person answers the way they do. Anyone who feels unable to answer says 'pass' and gives the card to the next person. When all the questions have been answered the pack can be shuffled and they should pick again. Two rounds of this is probably enough. For younger children who have difficulties reading, the teacher can read each question. The idea is to encourage children to explore each other's views and feelings together, and to begin to get to know each other more personally.

Debriefing questions: Which question got 'passed' the most? Were there any questions that no one was willing to answer? Did groups express different views? Did everyone in the group take turns?

Task 4.2 – Predicaments

Time: Twenty minutes to one hour.
Group size: Stable groups (fours).
Briefing: Encourage children to answer the questions as openly as possible, to listen to each other's answers and to ask 'why' questions to get reasons. They could also think about what they should do and then what they actually would do.
Task: Place the pile of prepared cards from Worksheet 4b in the centre of the group.

1   Explain that each person in turn will take a card from the pile. They will read out what is written on the card and then say what they would do in the situation described on the card. If someone does not want to answer a particular card they may say 'pass' and take the next card. The rejected card is placed in the unused pile.
2   The first person takes a card and reads out the predicament, for example, 'Your house is on fire. You have time to save two things.' The group can then make comments and a discussion may follow. Keep reminding the group there may be more than one possible answer (and answers are not necessarily correct). Encourage them to explore the reasons given.
3   Continue the process until everyone has had one or more goes. Groups could suggest their own predicaments for other groups to discuss. You do not need to use all the cards but, if you don't, make sure you select a range of positive and negative scenarios.

Debriefing questions: How did people answer the question about the person who had collapsed on the pavement? Were they being honest with themselves? Would they really behave like that? What did they learn about themselves? What did they learn about other people? Were some questions harder to discuss than others?

Task 4.3 – 'This week I've noticed that ...'

Time: Ten to fifteen minutes.

Group size: Whole class, groups or both.

Briefing: Encourage children to think of something nice or positive to say about another person in their group.

Task: Ask children to volunteer to make a positive comment in front of the whole class (or the rest of the group) about another group or classmate. The sentence has to start 'This week I've noticed that ...' or 'This week I'm pleased that ...'. Some children will have difficulties in finding a peer to praise. To overcome this you could choose one for them. Teachers should ensure that all children are mentioned. This task can be done on a regular basis at the end of a day or week.

Debriefing: Encourage children to build on these developments. Discuss whether hearing other people say positive things about you affects your confidence. Ensure everyone is included. Encourage pupils to find something positive in difficult situations, such as conflicts or fallings-out.

Worksheet 4a: Sample questions for the truth game

What do you do best?	What sort of TV programmes do you like?
If you won a thousand pounds, what would you spend it on?	What makes you laugh the most?
Who do you like most in the group?	What was your happiest moment?
When was the last time you cried?	What do you think the group needs to do better?
What angered you most last week?	What lie have you told recently?
What scares you the most?	What embarrasses you?

Worksheet 4b: Predicaments

What would you do if ...?

You are accused of stealing some money by a police officer. You did not do it but you know who did.	While in a supermarket you accidentally knock over a pyramid of cans on display. They go everywhere and everyone is looking.
A friend offers you a stolen video at a very low price.	Someone seems to be following you. There is no one else around.
Your house is on fire. You have time to save two things.	You find a person lying on a busy pavement. She could be ill or drunk. Other people are stepping over her.
Someone keeps picking on your best friend.	You see two young men hitting a policeman.
A friend asks you for advice because they have accidentally made a deep scratch with a bike pedal along the side of their dad's brand new car.	You lend five pounds to a friend. Repayment was promised for last Wednesday. Your friend seems to be avoiding you and has not paid back any money.
You have been invited to a friend's birthday party this evening but you also have maths homework that has to be done by tomorrow.	You have one pound to spend in the shop at lunchtime. You can buy yourself either a healthy sandwich or a packet of crisps and a chocolate bar.
You are planning your birthday party and you can have either a clown or a magician, but not both.	Your mum wants you to help her make a cake but your younger sister is having problems with her homework and you can help her understand it. There is only time to do one or the other.
On your birthday you are given a present you already have.	Someone is spreading lies about you.

Unit 5

Becoming a good listener

PRIMARY

Resources

You will need two working ears ... and Teacher information sheet 5a.

Learning objectives

- To think about what it means to be a good listener
- To identify what good listening looks and sounds like
- To practise being a good listener

Briefing – whole class work (twenty minutes)

Briefly discuss listening skills, possibly using the following questions:

- Why is it important to listen?
- How does it feel when people do not listen to you?
- How does it feel when people interrupt or talk over you?

Demonstrate poor listening with a child volunteer as the speaker talking about 'What I did at the weekend' and yourself as the listener. Then demonstrate active listening, which might involve:

- engaging with a pupil in a conversation about their favourite sport;
- establishing and maintaining appropriate eye contact;
- nodding and saying 'uh-huh';
- asking clarification questions or for more detail; and/or
- incorporating your own interest in the topic being discussed: for example, 'I used to be a great football player - I really loved it', then continue discussing your joint interest.

Ask pupils to turn to a partner and discuss the differences between you as poor listener and as active listener, in terms of what you did and did not do (three minutes). Then have a *class discussion* about the two situations. Some questions you might ask:

- What was the difference between the two situations?
- What things indicated/'told you' that I was not listening?
- What did I do when I was actively listening?
- What could [the speaker] have done to make me listen or find out whether I was listening or not?

Group work (ten minutes)

Brainstorm in fours the things people say and do when they are actively listening in a group. Note these in a 'T' chart (see below). Which are the most important ones? The children could also draw up a 'T' chart of poor listening behaviour. Select a scribe for each group to note down the ideas.

Good listener

Sounds like	Looks like
'Uh-huh', 'yes', ask questions, etc.	Maintain eye contact, nod, etc.

Figure 5.1 An example of a 'T' chart

Feedback to the class (five to ten minutes)

Ask two groups to feed back their ideas to the class and note these on a large sheet of paper. Ask other groups whether they came up with any different ideas. Discuss these to ensure they are examples of active listening and narrow down to the five most important in each column (see Teacher information sheet 5a).

Group work – practise listening (fifteen minutes)

In fours, give pupils an opportunity to practise their listening skills. Each group should split into a speaker, two listeners and an observer. The speaker should spend a few minutes talking about one of the topics below. The listeners practise their skills and the observer watches and notes down the listening skills used and how often. After a couple of minutes swap roles to give all pupils a turn at practising their listening, speaking and observing skills.
   Suggested topics:

- What I like doing in my spare time
- How I would change the school if I had the chance
- If I could control all the money in the world, I would ...
- How I would redesign the playground

Debriefing (ten minutes)

Discuss how easy it was to listen. Did listeners use all the skills identified? Add any new listening skills to the 'T' chart. Discuss what speakers might say to ensure listeners are paying attention and understand what is being said. Encourage children to use their listening skills and to remind each other to use them. *Discuss any rules that pupils would like to add to a list of class rules for group talk.*

Teacher information sheet 5a: Becoming a good listener

Below are some ideas about what makes a good listener. Some of these are more complex than others but, taking into consideration the children in your class, try to ensure that pupils identify most of the following points:

Good listening behaviour:

- Maintaining eye contact, nodding, smiling at the right time, shaking the head at the right time, looking surprised, etc.
- Saying 'yes', 'yeah', 'mm-hm', 'uh-huh', etc.
- Responding – 'Wow', 'That's funny', 'That sounds really great', 'Oh dear', 'Oh really?', 'Right, okay', 'Cool', 'Hee hee', 'That's interesting', 'Good idea', 'Oh well', 'That's life', etc.
- Asking for clarification – 'I don't understand', 'What do you mean?', 'Which one?', 'How?', 'Why?', 'When?', etc.
- Don't take the focus of the conversation away from the speaker by disagreeing or talking about yourself (unless your point introduces other reasons for being interested in the subject).
- Respond to the feelings that may lie behind the speaker's words. Show that you understand how the speaker feels.
- Don't rush to fill silences. Sit out pauses to encourage the speaker to resume talking.
- Use open-ended questions to encourage the speaker to continue talking or to elaborate.
- Don't 'finish off' what the speaker is saying by interpreting what you think they are trying to say. You might be wrong!

Things speakers can say to ensure someone is listening:

- 'Do you know what I mean?'
- 'Have you ever had that happen to you?'
- 'What do you think?'

Listening, asking questions and giving instructions

LOWER PRIMARY

Learning objectives

- To develop good listening skills
- To help children to give accurate descriptions

Briefing – Whole class work (five minutes)

Ask everyone to think about what they did after school yesterday. All children should be able to recall, but you should encourage pupils to think of three specific things that they did. Put a few examples on the board to stimulate ideas. Encourage children to ask questions of each other. Remind them that there are no right or wrong answers. When finishing the task, each partner should be able to report to the rest of the class one of their partner's activities.

Paired work – three things (ten minutes)

Pairs of children are asked to tell their partner three activities that they did between leaving school yesterday and returning to school today. When one partner completes her/his description, the other relates their three activities. Jointly, the partners should then decide one interesting (or unusual, usual, etc.) activity that each undertook. The teacher then calls the whole class together, and children report on their partner's activity.

Debriefing (five minutes)

With the class, the teacher should emphasise listening and support skills. Discuss how easy it was to listen. Did listeners ask questions? Explore what happened between partners if one of the pair could not remember. How did the pairs decide which one activity to report?

UPPER PRIMARY

Resources

One sheet of paper and a pen for each child. Teacher information sheet 6a. Figures 6.1 to 6.4.

Learning objectives

- To think further about good listening skills
- To help children give accurate instructions
- To help children ask relevant questions for clarification
- To illustrate the effectiveness of two-way communication

Briefing – Whole class work (ten minutes)

Recap active listening skills. Make the point that sometimes listeners do not understand and have to ask questions to gain clarification. Emphasise that communication also involves being a good speaker (and listener) and this is important when giving instructions.

Task (ten minutes)

One-way communication task: One child is asked to come to the front to instruct the class in drawing a figure made of squares (Figure 6.1). (Teacher shows only that child the figure.) *The class cannot ask questions or talk to the speaker.* When finished, ask the children to compare what they have drawn with the drawing made by the person next to them. Find out how many people got the drawing right. What were the most common misinterpretations? What could the speaker have done/ said to help you understand better? Explain why you have to be explicit.

Two-way communication task: Next, a different child is asked to instruct the class to draw another figure (Figure 6.2). (Teacher shows only that child the figure.) She/he faces the class and the class *may ask questions*. When finished, ask the children to compare what they have drawn with the drawing made by the person next to them. Find out how many people got the drawing exactly right and compare this to the success rate in the one-way task. Ask pairs to think about the differences between the two situations.

Class discussion (ten minutes)

Use Teacher information sheet 6a for discussion. The teacher should note class responses to questions 5 and 6 and save for future reference.

Tasks

The two following activities may be used separately across two sessions or concurrently in one session.

Group work – 'Living sculpture' (ten to fifteen minutes)

Resources: Floor space.

Time: Twenty minutes or more.

Group size: Combine two stable groups together.

Briefing: How will each group decide who will be the leader and the modeller? Listen carefully to the instructions given by the modeller.

Task: (You might want to have a class demonstration of the activity before doing the activity in groups.) The activity requires a modeller and a leader. The modeller is required to sit or stand with his back to the others while they form a standing circle and hold hands. The leader should now give each person a number – 1 to 7 (or so) – and ask the modeller to shout out action instructions along the lines of: 'No. 4, lift up No. 1's leg'; 'No. 3, put your arm round No. 6's neck'; 'No. 2, crawl through No. 4's legs', etc. The group's hands must remain linked for as long as is humanly possible, and at some point (preferably prior to the collapse of the group in a heap in the middle of the floor!), the modeller should be instructed by the leader to turn round and view the 'living sculpture' he or she has created.

Some 'modellers' may need help in thinking up appropriate instructions and it is important that adult help is offered if ideas do not come spontaneously from the group. The sequence can be repeated several times.

Debriefing: How did it go? What was the hardest part? What made it a success? What could you do next time to make it more successful?

Paired work – 'Escape from Wotu Island' (fifteen minutes)

Resources: Copies of Figures 6.3 for half the class and Figure 6.4 for the other half.

Group size: Pairs from the stable groups.

Scenario: En route to Central America, while flying over the Bermuda Triangle, the engines on your plane cut out. Fortunately, you managed to parachute out of the plane with your radio transmitter before it crashed into the sea. You have floated down and landed in the northern part of a remote island in the middle of the Atlantic Ocean renowned for its inhospitable environment. If the resident crocodiles catch you, they'll certainly eat you! Using your radio, you contact air traffic control and they tell you that they will rescue you from the south of the island, but first you will have to get from the north to the south using the map you have and instructions from the flight controller. The flight controller will guide you around some of the dangerous obstacles in your way. To succeed, all you have to do is stay alive!

Task: Split the class into equal numbers of flight controllers and pilots and then pair them up. Outline the scenario and then give a copy of Figure 6.3 to each pilot and Figure 6.4 to each flight controller. Ask flight controllers and pilots to sit facing each other with a book behind their sheet. *Children must not look at their partner's map.* The flight controller should guide the pilot across the island to the rescue point while avoiding dangerous obstacles. The pilot should draw the route that he/she takes on the map. When they have finished, compare their maps to see if the pilot has survived. Unfortunately, the two maps are old and slightly different from each other: some of the dangers are marked on one map but not on the other. So flight controllers and pilots will need to be very careful and make sure their communication is two way.

Debriefing (ten minutes): Ask the class about:

- the strategies they used to solve the problem;
- the problems they encountered;
- how they clarified what the flight controller meant;
- the sorts of questions that provided useful information; and
- the sorts of descriptions that were most accurate.

How might pupils change their behaviour when helping classmates, based on what they experienced in this exercise? Encourage children to use their listening, questioning and explaining skills when working on activities at other times, for example during class time. *Discuss any rules that pupils would like to add or amend in their list of class rules for group talk.*

Teacher information sheet 6a: Listening, asking questions and giving instructions

1   Which exercise (Figure 6.1 or Figure 6.2) took less time? Why?
2   In which exercise did people *think* they did better? Why do they feel more confident in that exercise?
3   In which exercise did people *actually* do better? Why did more people do better in that exercise?
4   Which exercise was less frustrating for the person giving the instructions? Why wasn't it frustrating for them? Which exercise was less frustrating for those listening? Why?
5   What are the advantages and disadvantages of one-way communication?

Advantages	Disadvantages

6   What are the advantages and disadvantages of two-way communication?

Advantages	Disadvantages

7   How were these exercises like some situations you have been in or seen? Such as: trying to communicate with someone who does not speak your language very well; watching a cookery programme on TV and then trying to make the dish, or following another type of demonstration on TV; trying to follow a teacher's directions.

Source: Farivar and Webb, 1991
(see Useful references and resources, p. 99)

One-way communication

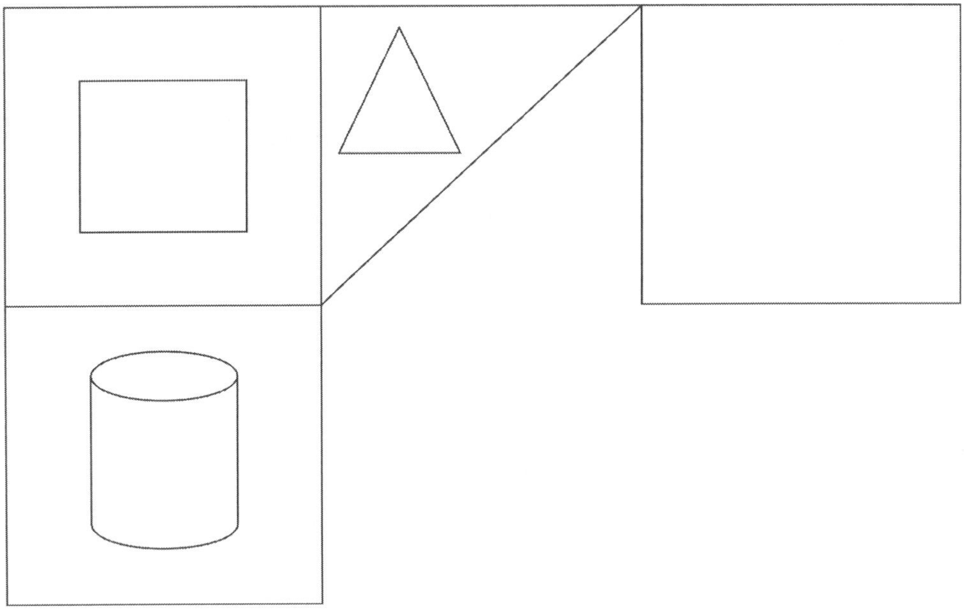

Figure 6.1

✂ - ✂ - ✂

Two-way communication

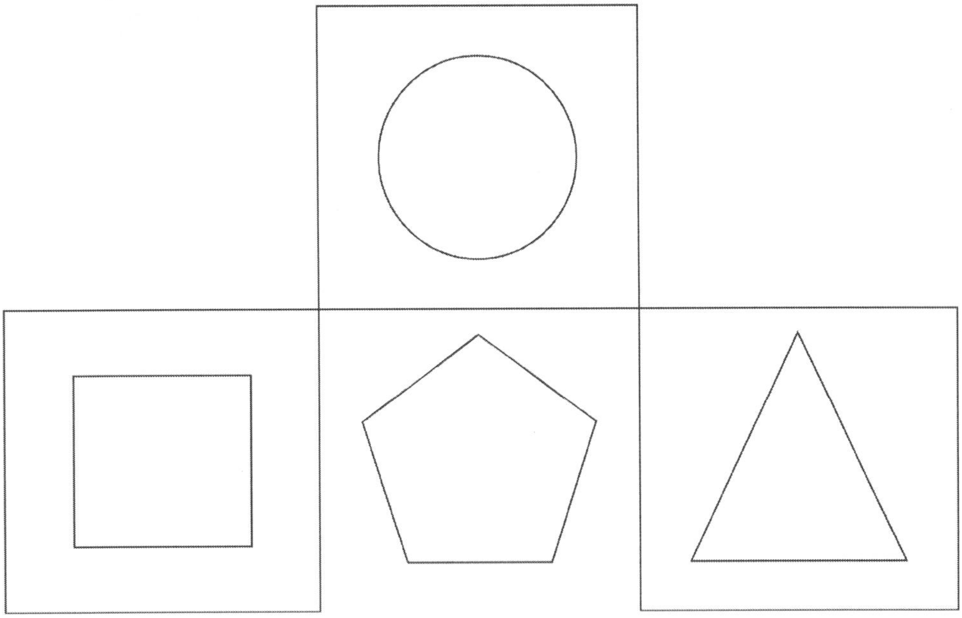

Figure 6.2

Pilot's instructions

- The flight controller will direct you to the rescue point.
- Tell the flight controller about the dangerous obstacles on your map.
- DO NOT LOOK AT THE FLIGHT CONTROLLER'S MAP!
- Draw the route on your map.
- Good luck in your adventure!

You must avoid:

- the quick sand
- Crocodile River
- the haunted forest
- Piranha River
- the bandits
- the bottomless pit
- the volcano
- the pirate village

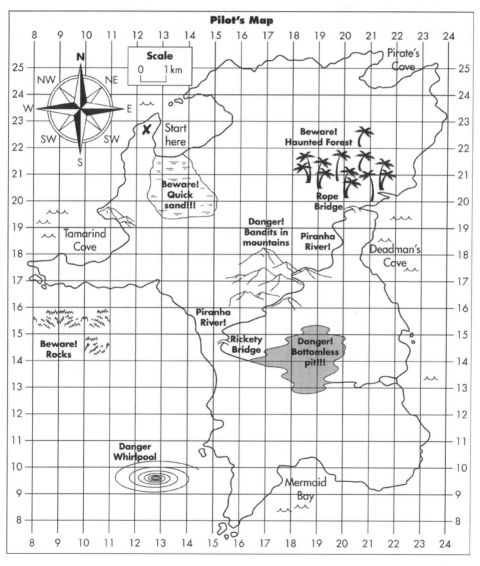

Figure 6.3 Pilot's map

Flight controller's instructions

- You must direct the pilot to the rescue point.
- Beware of the dangers on your map and on the pilot's map.
- The pilot will tell you what dangerous obstacles are on their map.
- DO NOT LOOK AT THE PILOT'S MAP!
- Good luck in the adventure!

Guide the pilot, but:

- avoid the quick sand
- avoid Crocodile River
- avoid the haunted forest
- avoid Piranha River

- avoid the bandits
- avoid the bottomless pit
- avoid the volcano
- avoid the pirate village

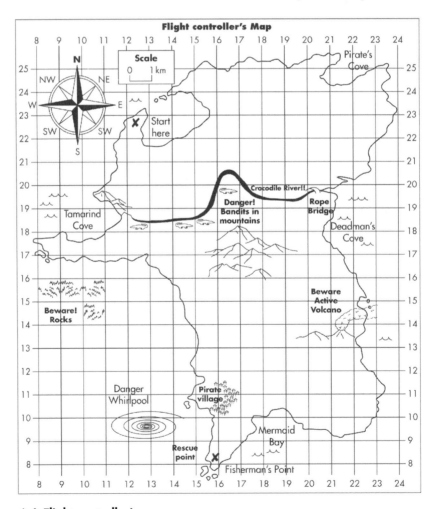

Figure 6.4 Flight controller's map

Helping skills

LOWER PRIMARY

Resources

You will need an A4-sized photocopy of rabbit (or similar animal, or an object such as a tree, car, etc.). Enough copies of the rabbit should be made so that each child in the class has one. Each copy of the rabbit is then cut into four random pieces (with older children, it can be cut into a greater number of pieces) so that no two copies of the rabbit are cut into the same pieces. Pieces from two copies of the rabbit are then put into a single envelope (hence thirty rabbits, fifteen envelopes).

Learning objectives

- To think about what it means to be an effective helper/collaborator
- To understand that sharing resources and ideas is the best way to help
- To understand that explanations are often important for success and that any individual child cannot simply assert her/his own view

Briefing – whole class work (five to ten minutes)

Introduce and explain the lesson objectives above. Remind the pupils of the two lessons that focused on listening skills, asking questions and giving instructions (Units 5 and 6). Emphasise the importance of these skills when helping others.

Task (ten to fifteen minutes)

The task can be undertaken in pairs or groups of four. Each pair of children is given an envelope. Whether the children undertake the task in pairs or fours, the teacher asks the children to open the envelope and place the pieces of the rabbit in the centre of the table (where they are sitting). Pairs/groups are then asked to assemble complete pictures of the rabbit.

Debriefing (ten minutes)

Discuss how the children pieced together and shared the construction of the rabbit between partners. What happened if one child tried to dominate the assembly of the rabbits? Did the pairs/groups take turns in choosing pieces? Did the children find it useful talking through their problems? How will they try to help each other in the future? Encourage children to practise and use helping skills during normal class lessons and to remind each other when they are not being helpful. *Discuss any rules that pupils would like to add or amend in their list of class rules for group talk.*

UPPER PRIMARY

Resources

Teacher information sheets 7a and 7b, Worksheets 7c and 7d, Pieces of string for pupils to learn how to tie different types of knot (see Teacher information sheet 7b).

Learning objectives

- To think about what it means to be an effective helper/collaborator
- To understand that guiding someone through an activity is the best way to help
- To understand that explanations are often important for success

Briefing – whole class work (twenty minutes)

Introduce and explain the lesson objectives above. Remind the pupils of the lesson that focused on clarifying and asking questions, giving feedback and being a good listener (Unit 6). Emphasise the importance of these skills when helping others. Have a short discussion on the following issues:

- What is helping?
- Why do I need to be helped when I can copy?
- When I am helping someone, why can't I just give them the answer, tell them what to do or do it for them?
- What do we do when we give effective help?

It is important to recognise that helping is also beneficial for the person doing the helping since they must verbalise their thinking in simple ways for the help to be effective. This aids and develops learning and understanding.

In the ensuing discussion two questions you might ask are:

- What things indicated that I was not helping?
- What would I have done if I had been trying to be helpful?

Illustrate through a demonstration and discussion the important distinction between the following different methods of giving help (you could use Teacher information sheet 7b with examples of how to tie a figure-of-eight knot and a bowline):

- *Showing* someone how to do something before they do the activity: for example, figure of eight knot
- *Telling* someone how to do something before they do the activity
- *Guiding* someone through the activity as they do it: that is, telling, showing and explaining as the person works through the activity

Finally, emphasise the importance (in certain circumstances, such as helping with a maths problem) of the helper asking the person who needs the help to explain what they have done or how they have done something before help is given. This means you can see where the person in need of help has gone wrong.

Paired work – 'explaining problems to each other' (ten to fifteen minutes)

Give half of the class the mathematics problems on Worksheet 7c and the other half those on Worksheet 7d. (If these are too simple or too difficult, pick some other real-life mathematical problems that are more suitable.) After pupils have managed to answer some of the questions, pair them up so that each member of the pair has answered different questions. The pair should take it in turns to explain how to solve one of their problems. Then they should explain to their partner each step in the calculation: what they did first, what they did next and so on. They should not just give the answer ('It's fifty-four') or simplify their methodology ('It's six times nine.').

If problems arise, get pupils to ask their partner how to do the calculation. The pupil in need of help should remember to explain how they tried to do the problem so that the helper can identify where they went wrong. If some children finish more quickly than others, you might like to teach them how to tie a bowline (see Teacher information sheet 7b).

Debriefing (five to ten minutes)

Discuss how easy/hard it was for the children to explain the problems and to break them down for their partners. Did they find it useful talking through the problems? How will they try to help each other in the future? Encourage children to practise and use helping skills during normal class lessons and to remind each other when they are not being helpful. *Discuss any rules that pupils would like to add or adjust in their list of class rules for group talk*.

Follow-up work

There are many construction material kits used in school classrooms these days (e.g. LEGO®, QUADRO®) and these can be used along with the two main roles of adviser (helper) and builder (the person being helped). The adviser reads the instructions and may select the appropriate materials/ pieces that are to be used and directs the builder on how to combine them to produce the model. Children can use the given instructions or create their own models and instructions to be used by others.

Another way to integrate helping alongside more collaborative work is to get pupils devising Mathematical problems for each other to solve, as follows:

1   Pupils devise problems (possibly maths problems) in pairs.
2   Pass problems to the next pair along the line, who try to solve them.

3   Pass problems back to the original pair for marking.

4   One member from each pair explains to one member from the next pair where that pair went wrong (presuming that they did go wrong!).

5   The pairs reform and the one child explains to their partner where they went wrong.

Teacher information sheet 7a: Being a good helper

Below are some ideas about what being a good helper 'looks like' and 'sounds like'. Some of these are more complex than others, but taking into consideration the children in your class, try to ensure that pupils identify most of the following points:

Good helping behaviour:

- Notice when others need help (look around in your group and see if anyone might need help).
- Tell others to ask you if they need help.
- When someone asks you for help, help them.
- Encourage the person to explain what they have done so far or how they did it.
- Be a good listener: let the person explain what help they need.
- Do not give the answer or do the task for the person; rather, guide them through it.
- Give explanations so that the person understands why they should do something in a particular way.
- Watch while the person tries to do the task themself; guide them if necessary.
- Give specific feedback on how the problem/task was tackled.
- Praise the person when they have tried and succeeded in doing the task.
- Check they have understood why this was the best way to solve the problem.

Things helpers can say to make sure people who need help know they are willing to assist:

- If you need help, ask me.
- Of course I'll help you. What help do you need?
- Tell me what you've done so far.
- How did you do this?
- Let me explain the way I would do this.
- Why don't you have a go now and I'll watch you do it.
- You got up to this part right. Now this is where you went wrong.
- Well done, I think you've got it!
- Tell me how you would do this the next time.
- You're a star!

Teacher information sheet 7b: Helping skills

If you are not familiar with these knots, it is advisable to practise them a few times first.

The figure-of-eight knot

1   First make a loop in front of you
2   Put your hand behind and through the back of the loop so that you can see the pads of your fingers and palm and so the bottom part of the loop is touching against your knuckles on the back of your hand.
3   Twist your hand so your fingers move away from you and point vertically as if you are inspecting your fingernails. Now you see your fingernails. Grab hold of the end of the string and pull it through the loop – drawing your hand out of the knot in the process.
4   You now have a figure-of-eight knot.

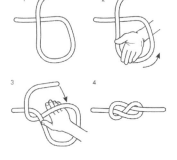

If you double the string up from the start, you can make it so that you have a loop at the end.

The bowline

The bowline (pronounced 'bo-lin') is a really handy knot because of its great strength and the ease with which it can be undone, even when it has been put under great tension. It also does not slip. It can be used in lots of different situations: climbers, sailors and firemen all use this knot. The only drawback is that it is difficult to learn how to tie when using the traditional method. Try this version instead:

1   Create a 'rabbit hole' as in the diagram. Pass the end of the rope around (or through) the object being tied to (marked as 'x').
2   The 'rabbit' (the end of the string) then comes out of its 'hole', goes around the 'tree' (the farthest string, and leading away, from the object being tied to), then back into its 'hole'.
3   You now have a bowline knot.

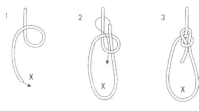

Worksheet 7c: Real-life mathematical problems

When working out the answers, think about what you do first, second and so on until you have completed the problem.

1   There are twelve sweets in each packet. How many sweets are there in six packets?

2   Brian has four CD towers. Each tower has thirty-five CDs. How many CDs does Brian have in total?

3   Harjeet has read one-eighth of her magazine. She has read to page twelve. How many pages does her magazine have?

Worksheet 7d: Real-life mathematical problems

When working out the answers, think about what you do first, second and so on until you have completed the problem.

1   Clare is 27. Her mother is nineteen years older. How old is Clare's mother?

2   Three-quarters of the thirty-two people in a supermarket are adults. How many are children?

3   Tariq has read to page fifty-four of his book. He needs to read twenty-one more pages to reach halfway. How many pages does Tariq's book have?

Group discussion
Giving reasons and weighing ideas

LOWER PRIMARY

Learning objectives

- To help children understand that they need to give reasons that underlie their ideas.
- To help children understand that they need to weigh the reasons and evidence for and against an idea.
- To encourage children to practise giving and asking for reasons.

Briefing (five to ten minutes)

Introduce and explain the lesson objectives and emphasise the importance of speaking and listening in relation to explanations and giving reasons. Refer children back to previous group-work tasks where they have had to make decisions.

Group work (ten to fifteen minutes)

Working in pairs, children are asked where they might like to go for a class visit. The pairs should be encouraged to make a short list (between two and four) of places to visit. When the children have put together their lists, each pair should then say why the class might like to visit each of the places. If there is time, the teacher can encourage each pair to choose one 'best' place to visit, and explain why they made this choice. Following these discussions, a whole class session can be used to identify the range of places to visit.

Debriefing (five to ten minutes)

Review with the class how they came to identify the range of class visits. Then ask the children to review whether it was difficult to provide reasons for each visit. Ask the children to reflect on why it is important to give reasons for choices and suggestions.

UPPER PRIMARY

Resources

Teacher information sheet 8a is primarily for your benefit, but the phrases can be discussed with pupils.

Learning objectives

- To help children understand why they need to give reasons for ideas and the importance of weighing the reasons and evidence for and against an idea.
- To encourage children to practise giving and asking for reasons and to think about evidence for and against ideas.

Briefing – whole class work (ten minutes)

Introduce and explain the lesson objectives and recap about speaking and listening in relation to explanations and giving reasons. Refer children back to previous group-work tasks where they have had to make decisions. In these situations children were encouraged to give reasons for their ideas. Ask the children to think back to how and why this was useful and then discuss the following:

- What 'reasons' are
- Why it is important that we give reasons
- What we say when we give and ask for reasons during group discussion (see Teacher information sheet 8a)
- What giving reasons helps us to do

Explain that, when discussing an issue, giving reasons and weighing the evidence for *and against* an idea helps others understand how we see things and helps us to make better decisions and solve problems.

Group work – having a debate (thirty-five minutes or longer – see Follow-up work)

This task is complex, so you are advised to break it down into stages. In this way, the pupils will be able to focus on what they are doing at the moment, rather than on the complexities of what they will have to do next. You should emphasise to pupils that you hope to hear them using some of the phrases listed on Teacher information sheet 8a during their discussions throughout the activity.

- Step 1 (ten minutes): Split the class into equal numbers of pairs. Select one (or more) of the controversial topics listed below. Half of the pairs are to identify three (or more) opinions and their associated reasons in favour of the statement - the other half, a similar number of opinions and associated reasons against the statement. The pairs should note down their arguments.

- Step 2 (fifteen minutes): Combine pairs that are 'for' with those that are 'against' to form groups of four. These groups then report their arguments to each other and discuss them, trying to find ways to counter each other's arguments. They should note down any criticisms next to the ideas they came up with.
- Step 3 (ten minutes): Ask the groups to have a full discussion to decide on the correctness of the statement and to note the reasons why they reached the conclusion they did. If pupils are not able to decide after ten minutes, allow them to agree to disagree (you may be there a long time otherwise!).

Choose from the following controversial topics:

- Hunting foxes is inhumane.
- Zoos are good places for animals.
- Being in the circus is a good life for both humans and animals.
- Dropping litter keeps people in a job.
- Recycling is a good thing.
- Saving energy is a waste of time.
- Watching horror movies makes people more violent.
- Children should be allowed to stay up late to watch TV.
- Playing violent console games makes people more aggressive.

Debriefing questions

- How well did they report arguments for and against ideas?
- When they discussed the arguments for and against, did they feel as though they were going around in circles?
- Did they find that this helped them weigh alternative ideas more successfully?
- Were the groups able to agree on whether the original statement was correct?
- How did they resolve disputes? Did they have to agree to disagree?
- How would they do things differently next time?

Encourage pupils to give reasons for their thinking and explanations when doing group work in other lessons. *Discuss any rules that pupils would like to add or amend in their list of class rules for group talk.*

Follow-up work

After the debate activity, each group could compile a report exploring some of the arguments for and against, and the criticisms of these arguments.

Groups could devise and perform a simple role-play scene where the arguments for and against are acted out or explored.

The views on the controversial topic could be prepared as speeches or articles for a newspaper in a persuasive, evaluative or informative format.

Teacher information sheet 8a: Phrases often used to provide reasoning during group work

Sounds like	Communicative action
'Why?'	Requests reason
'Maybe ... because ...'	Suggestion plus reason
'How about ... because ...'	Suggestion plus reason
'I think ... because ...'	Opinion plus reason
'No, that can't be right because ... so ...'	Exploring implications of an argument.
'If ... then ...'	Exploring reasoning
'Yes ... but ...'	Giving reasons against an idea
'No ... because ...'	Giving reasons against an idea
'But what about ...?'	Raising alternative interpretations
'I understand your point of view but ...'	Raising alternative interpretations
'I can see why you think that is a good idea but consider this ...'	Raising alternative interpretations

Group discussion
Making suggestions and speculating

LOWER PRIMARY

Resources

For each group class teachers will need one large sheet of drawing (or writing) paper and enough pencils for each member of the group. The task described below is known as 'co-operative drawing', so children will need space to lay out their paper to undertake any drawing.

Learning objectives

- To encourage children to use and think about reasons and reasoning in talk
- To think about the process of making suggestions and speculating
- To encourage children to practise making suggestions and speculating

Briefing (five to ten minutes)

Introduce and explain the lesson objectives and emphasise the importance of considering what can be drawn, agreeing who will draw what on the paper, and considering alternative objects to draw. Refer back to previous work on giving reasons for and against ideas, making suggestions and speculating. Remind children that when they have worked on group-work tasks they have often had to make group decisions.

Group work (fifteen minutes)

Give pairs (later this can be undertaken in small groups) one sheet of paper and two pencils. Ask them to make a drawing related to a current classroom topic (Tudor house, mini-beasts/insects, etc.). Before each pair begins the drawing, however, suggest that they agree what to draw and (perhaps) who should do which part of the drawing. As children become more competent with this activity, you can introduce colour and more complicated objects to draw.

Debriefing questions (five to ten minutes)

- How well did the pairs work together?
- Were they able to agree what to draw?
- Did they make suggestions about to what to draw?

UPPER PRIMARY

Resources

Worksheet 9a and Teacher information sheet 9b.

Learning objectives

- To encourage children to use and think about reasons and reasoning in talk
- To think about the process of making suggestions and speculating
- To encourage children to practise making suggestions and speculating

Briefing – whole class work (fifteen to twenty minutes)

Introduce and explain the lesson objectives and then recap what the class did in the lesson on giving reasons and weighing up ideas (Unit 8). Tell pupils that another important skill in group work is to be able to suggest alternative ideas and to speculate as to why something may be the case.

- Suggestions (five to ten minutes): When we engage in *brainstorming* the point is to come up with lots of different *possible* ideas. These ideas are only suggestions, and we may decide that some are better than others. Carry out a brainstorming session asking for suggestions for the following scenario: 'We have been given ten pounds by our headteacher. What shall we spend the money on?' Ask pupils to make suggestions about how the money could be spent. Emphasise that we all have our personal preferences and we could argue for ever, but the idea is to try to find something that we all might like. Encourage more tentative suggestions rather than definite advice/opinions. For example, encourage pupils to say, 'Maybe ...', 'You could ...', 'How about ...?', rather than 'I think ...', 'We will ...', 'We should ...'. You could finish off the activity by requesting reasons for and against the different ideas and then conclude with a vote.
- Speculating (five to ten minutes): Speculating is more about finding explanations for why something *might* happen - we use these in science. You could ask your pupils to speculate about one or two of the following questions (it does not matter if they are right or wrong - just get them to give an explanation.):
  - Why can we see stars only when it is dark or nearly dark?
  - Why does the moon seem to change shape?
  - Why do we see the moon only when it is dark or nearly dark?
  - If the world is round, why don't people at the bottom fall off?
  - Do people in Australia see everything upside down?

Group work – 'Lost in space' (fifteen minutes)

In their stable groups of four, two children in each group should take on the roles of scribe and chairperson (to ensure everyone presents their ideas and provides reasons). The others have a main responsibility for coming up with ideas and developing them.

Distribute a copy of Worksheet 9a to the scribe in each group and ask them to read out the scenario to the group. Groups must decide which five items they would save from the wreckage of the spaceship before it explodes. *Everyone in the group must have an opportunity to suggest and speculate*; it is up to the chairperson to enforce this. The group should consider each item in turn and discuss the evidence for and against saving it. The scribe could make notes on a piece of scrap paper. The scribe in each group should note down on Worksheet 9a the five items that the group finally decides they will save and the reasons why. The group should also decide what else it should do: for example, remain where it is or attempt to reach the space camp.

When each group has finished, the class should discuss the ideas and reasons for and against saving each item from the wreckage. A class answer should be sought and then compared to that suggested by NASA experts (see Teacher information sheet 9b).

Debriefing questions (five to ten minutes)

- How well did they get on with making suggestions and speculating? Did this help?
- Did they report reasons for and against these ideas?
- Did they find that this helped them make better decisions?
- How did you resolve disputes?
- How would you do things differently next time?

Encourage children to practise and use making suggestions and speculating during normal class lessons. *Discuss any rules that pupils would like to add or amend in their list of class rules for group talk.*

Worksheet 9a: Lost in space

You were in a spaceship travelling to the moon. Unfortunately, the spaceship has malfunctioned and crash-landed on the moon. You and your group are the only people to survive. It will take five days for Mission Control to prepare and send another spaceship to rescue you. There is a space camp six days' walk away. A couple of you have severe limb injuries but fortunately your space suits and air tanks (with a day's supply of air) are undamaged.

   Your spaceship is still on fire and is going to blow up. There is just time for you to save five things from this list of twelve items. You must decide as a group which items you are going to save. If you make the right decisions, you will survive. If you don't, you will perish!

- 1 box of matches
- 1 tube of food concentrate
- 1 portable gas heater
- 2 pistols
- 1 diet orange drink
- 1 telecommunications system (receiver and transmitter with solar batteries)
- 1 first aid box
- 2 oxygen cylinders (ten litres in each)
- 1 compass
- five litres water
- 3 signal flares (usable in a vacuum)
- 1 map of the moon

The chairperson must ensure that everyone has an opportunity and is encouraged to present their view. The scribe should note down the five items that the group decides to save and the reasons why these are so important.

- The most important item to save is ....
  because ....
- The second important item to save is...
  because ....
- The third important item to save is ....
  because ....
- The fourth important item to save is ....
  because ....
- The fifth important item to save is ....
  because ....

Teacher information sheet 9b: Lost in space

Groups should decide to remain where they are, as it will take longer to walk to the camp than for a rescue shuttle to arrive. Also, they do not know what dangers they may face on the long walk, which will be very difficult anyway, as some of them are injured. The group might decide to split up, with the healthy members walking to the camp and the injured ones remaining at the crash site. This is not recommended since it will be very difficult for any rescue mission to find them if they get lost or stuck.

The list below shows how important each object is for survival, according to NASA experts. To see how well the class has done, the points allocated to each object can be totalled by the teacher. Anything above 0 means they survive. (It may not be a good idea to total the points for each group as this may result in conflict between groups and some bragging that one group is doing better than others.)

1	Oxygen cylinders – there is no air in space	5
2	Water – there is no water on the moon	5
3	First aid box – to treat injuries from the crash	3
4	Food concentrate – there is no food on the moon	2
5	Telecommunication system – to communicate with Mission Control, to explain where you are and what has happened	2
6	Signal flares – to signal your location to rescuers	1
7	Map of the moon – might help you tell your rescuers where you are if you also have telecommunication system, although they would probably know better than you, since rockets are tracked	0
8	Pistols – what are you going to shoot (apart from each other when you are starving)?	-2
9	Diet orange drink – has few nutrients	-2
10	Heater – you are in a vacuum so the gas would not ignite, and you are wearing space suits so you will not get cold	-2
11	Compass – there is no magnetic north on the moon	-2
12	Matches – you are in a vacuum so the match will not light	-2

Unit 10

Group decisions
Reaching a consensus

LOWER PRIMARY

Resources

For each group teachers will need either a real (small) bag of sweets or a chocolate bar. Alternatively, you could photocopy (for each group) a bag of sweets or a chocolate bar. If you photocopy the bag of sweets, ensure that the number of sweets is identified on the bag or write the number on the photocopy.

Learning objectives

• To think about the process of making group decisions by reaching a consensus
• To practise making group decisions through consensus

Briefing (five to ten minutes)

Introduce and explain the lesson objectives and emphasise the importance of speaking and listening in relation to explanations and giving reasons. Refer back to the previous work on giving reasons for and against ideas, making suggestions and speculating. Remind children that when they have worked on group-work tasks they have often had to make group decisions. Making these decisions is not always easy but looking at the reasons for and against ideas helps the group make a decision.

Group work (ten minutes)

Working in pairs or small groups, each group is given a bag of sweets or a chocolate bar (or the photocopy). The children are asked how they can divide the sweets/chocolate among the group members. Groups may be encouraged to undertake a 'fair' distribution or agree another method of distribution. After each group has agreed a means of distribution, call the class back together and ask each group to report on their distribution. (It is optional whether you then allow the children to distribute and eat the sweets!)

Debriefing (five to ten minutes)

Review with the class how they came to distribute the sweets/chocolate. Then ask children to review whether it was difficult to decide on the means to distribute the sweets. Ask them to reflect on why it is important to give reasons for choices and suggestions.

Follow-up

If the discussion concerning distribution is too easy for the groups, try to find another object of 'value' to the children that may not be divided by a simple mathematical distribution (such as five sweets between four children) and ask them to undertake the discussion for distribution task.

UPPER PRIMARY

Resources

Worksheets 10a to 10d.

Learning objectives

- To think about the process of making group decisions by reaching a consensus
- To practise making group decisions through consensus

Briefing – Whole class work (twenty minutes)

Go over the learning objectives. Refer back to the previous work on giving reasons for and against ideas, making suggestions and speculating. Remind children that when they have worked on group-work tasks they have often made group decisions. Making these decisions is not always easy but looking at the reasons for and against ideas helps the group make a decision. This is done by finding the most sensible or logical reasons.

Discuss with your class the different ways of making decisions - voting by hand raising, private balloting and just asking if anyone disagrees/everyone agrees. In which situations would we use these and when would they be unsuitable? (Think about the number of people involved, the seriousness of the decision, the amount of money and time it might cost, the context, etc.) What are the problems with each form of reaching consensus? For example, a private ballot is time consuming and expensive. Public voting is formal and encourages conformity (especially if the question is hard, such as 'Who thinks the square root of 169 is 13?'). Asking if anyone disagrees is informal and encourages people to offer their view but only in small, familiar group situations. (Imagine a teacher asking the pupils this during assembly!)

Discourage pupils from voting when in small groups (this should be reserved for class discussion, etc.). Rather, they should make sure they have discussed the issues fully and that everyone has had an opportunity to have their say. Emphasise that when working in their groups they should always check that everyone has had a chance to say what they think and time to consider the issues. The phrases you can use to check that everyone is in agreement might be 'Are we all agreed?' or 'Can anyone think of a good reason why we shouldn't do/choose this?'

Group work – 'Best pet' (ten minutes)

In groups of four, use the information (see Worksheet 10a) to make decisions about which pet matches which owner. Groups should decide what should be done with the remaining pet. Upper primary pupils could prepare a case arguing why that pet should not be put down.

Group work – 'Best holiday' (ten minutes)

In groups of four, use the information (see Worksheet 10b) to make decisions about which holiday matches which person. Groups should outline their reasoning for each choice.

Group work – 'Who should be the class representative?' (twenty minutes)

In groups of four, use the information (see Worksheets 10c and 10d) to make a decision about which of the four pupils should be the class representative on the school council. Pupils should discuss the alternatives and then think about the criteria to use to select someone (e.g. ability to work with others, public speaking, being persuasive, confident).

Remind groups to use the ground rules for talk, to give reasons and counter-reasons to help weigh the alternative arguments. Groups may need to identify who will be spokesperson.

Debriefing questions (ten minutes or so)

- Who did they decide should become the class representative and for what reason?
- What criteria did they use for remaking this decision?
- Did they all agree?
- What did they do if they could not all agree?
- Did all groups suggest the same person? Why or why not?
- Do you think the class teacher will be pleased with your decisions? Why?
- Could a compromise decision be reached (e.g. sharing the position)?

Group work – 'Group debate' (ten minutes)

Your headteacher has been given some money to redevelop the playground but wants pupils to decide how the money should be spent. It can be spent on only one of the following:

- Building a wall down the middle of the playground so that the boys and girls can have separate play areas, and so that balls can be bounced against the wall
- Putting a roof on the playground so that it is always dry and warm
- Planting a hedge to encourage birds, animals and insects back into the area and making a quiet area

In fours, discuss which approach (questionnaire, debate, vote, survey) should be used to decide how the money should be spent. If two ideas are equally popular, how will this be resolved? Will it depend on cost, value for money or something else? The groups could also try to reach a consensus on one of the options for the playground. Are these good ideas? Are there better ones? A group spokesperson summarises the discussion and decision making.

Debriefing

Ask groups/pairs to evaluate how well they worked as a group and how they could improve on their group work if necessary (two minutes). Ask the class to evaluate how well they got on in terms of the particular skill discussed during the briefing. Do they have any new insights or strategies for how better to deal with this problem, etc.? Encourage children to practise making decisions during normal class lessons. *Discuss any rules that pupils would like to add or amend in their list of class rules for group talk.*

Worksheet 10a: Best pet

- A GP, often on call, who wants a pet that is low maintenance, tranquil and soothing
- A taxi driver doing shift work who likes learning about new things and collecting
- A checkout worker who has asthma and eczema and has to keep dust levels low at home
- An only child who needs bringing out of herself and wants a pet to share her worries and fears with

Parrot

Exotic fish

Cat

Dalmation dog

Pot-bellied pig

Worksheet 10b: Best holiday

- Retired widower who wants companionship and intellectual stimulation. Has a fear of flying but no time or cost limits.
- Single university student on a tight budget. Wants a good nightlife and likes to be active.
- Young newlyweds. Want late honeymoon in a romantic, exotic setting. Price limit because they've just bought a house, but want comfort and something memorable.
- Couple in their late thirties with twin teenage boys. Limited resources but must have a Saturday night away and no extra expenses. Boys like skateboarding; man likes looking at birds through his binoculars; woman wants to collapse by a pool with a good paperback.

Ski resort: Ante- and après-ski facilities (bars, cafés, clubs). All-in price, including hire of skis and ski passes. Spa hotel nearby where you can spend a day in Turkish steam rooms, have seaweed packs and massage.

Archaeological tour: Have to be fairly fit because the tour includes a lot of walking to sites that are inaccessible by coach. Price includes all meals but it is expensive. Field-notes sent before and background reading list given.

Cruise: Coach leaves from central London and meets ship at Dover. Route into the Baltic stopping at Riga, Tallinn, St Petersburg and Helsinki. Ship has hairdressers, swimming pools, cabaret and other entertainment, as well as kids' clubs, amusement arcade and quiz nights. All meals included but will need spending money aboard and ashore.

Club Mediterranean: Extinct volcanic island with camp on it. Basic accommodation, but lots of watersports: windsurfing, paragliding, water-skiing, snorkelling. Food included but not the extra activities.

Worksheet 10c: Who should be the class representative?

It is the beginning of another term and the headteacher of Ferryboat School has decided to set up a school council. The problem is that the teachers know that there are many children in their classes who would *enjoy* being the class representative but who might not be the *best pupil* to communicate the class's opinion on school matters. One teacher, Miss Langrick, has asked you to help her make this difficult decision. After a vote, the following *four* pupils had the same number of votes. She needs to choose just *one* person from the candidates.

   You must decide which pupil should be the class representative and explain why. You should also explain why the others should not be given the responsibility. When you have made a decision, complete the sentences below for each of the four children.

.... should not be made class representative

because ....

....

....

.... should not be made class representative

because ....

....

....

.... should not be made class representative

because ....

....

....

.... should be made class representative

because ....

....

....

Worksheet 10d: The candidates

Javid is a popular boy with many friends, mainly other boys. He likes to be the focus of attention and likes to get his own way. He is confident and good at speaking in front of a large audience. He is fairly good at group work but sometimes he ignores what the girls have to say and he is not very good at persuading people. He wants to be the class representative because it will mean he can miss lessons.

Maria is also popular, and has a mix of boy and girl friends. She likes to play a leading role without dominating other children and is good at working with others and persuading them. She is very conscious of the fact that she has a lisp. When she has to read out her work to the class her voice becomes very quiet, even though her writing is usually very interesting and she has good ideas. She doesn't want to be the class representative but her friends put her forward.

Aran is a very able boy who thinks a lot about things that are happening in the world. He has a few friends in the class. He is quiet in lessons and likes to get on with tasks on his own, although he can work well in a group. He is not a natural leader but when there are problem-solving tasks in science and maths he usually finds the best way to solve them. He is not bothered about being the class representative.

Raksha has one good friend, another girl, and they spend all their time together. They always want to sit next to each other and work together. They won't let other children play their games or share their secrets. But Raksha desperately wants to be the class representative. She is very confident but does not listen to what other people have to say, so few people listen to her.

More decision making

Consensus and compromise

UPPER PRIMARY

Resources

Worksheets 11a, 11b and 11c.

Learning objectives

- To think about the process of making group decisions by reaching a consensus
- To think about the process of making compromise decisions during group work when a unanimous decision cannot be reached
- To practise making group decisions through consensus

Briefing – whole class work (ten minutes)

Explain the learning objectives. Refer back to previous work on giving reasons, suggestions and coming to a consensus. Explore pupils' feelings about how easy or hard they found it in previous lessons to reach a consensus so that a decision could be made. If they found reaching a consensus difficult, explore ways in which they could overcome this problem. Get pupils to anticipate how they will deal with conflict if it arises.

Group work – 'Who should get the pay rise?' (fifteen minutes)

Put pupils into groups of four or six (an even number so that there is no easy majority) and give them Worksheet 11a. The groups should decide which employee should receive the pay rise. First they should think about the criteria to use to select someone. Give the groups ten to fifteen minutes to discuss the problem until they think they have made a decision. Remind the groups to use the ground rules for talk and remember to give reasons and counter-reasons to help weigh up the alternative arguments.

Group feedback (five minutes)

- Who did pupils decide should get the pay rise and for what reason?
- What criteria did they use for making a decision?
- Did all groups suggest the same person? Why not?
- Do you think the company will be pleased with your decision? Why?
- If a compromise was reached, would it be acceptable? For example, could the pay rise be shared between several employees?

Debriefing (five to ten minutes)

Ask children how easy it was to reach group decisions. Explore the different ways groups achieved (or failed to achieve) a consensus decision. Did they all discuss the reasons for and against the different ideas? What did they do when they could not agree? Did they have to come to a compromise? How did they do this? Encourage children to remember the successful decision-making strategies and to try to use them in the future when making decisions and resolving disagreement. *Discuss any rules that pupils would like to add or amend in their list of class rules for group talk.*

Follow-up work

Groups could consider the criteria they used to decide who should get the pay rise. Alternatively, they could identify a number of criteria - good at their work, have good ideas, problems at home, etc. - put ticks in the boxes, decide which criteria are the most important from different perspectives - the employer's, welfare, etc. - and then re-evaluate who should get the pay rise.

Group work – 'Floating and sinking' (fifteen minutes)

Give pupils Individual worksheet 11b and ask them to predict individually whether the different items will float or sink. After a few minutes put them into groups of four and ask them to compare their predictions. (Remind the groups that they should use the ground rules for group talking and remember to provide reasons.) Give each group Worksheet 11c and ask members to reach a consensus on which objects will float and their reasons why. Ask the groups to choose a spokesperson who will summarise their joint decision and reasons.

Groups that finish early might like to predict whether the objects would sink or float if the water is heated, if salt/oil is added to the water, if sugar is added to the water, or if the water is replaced with honey.

Give pupils the opportunity to test their predictions and then to reconvene as a group to explain where they went wrong and explore the reasons why.

Worksheet 11a: Who should get the pay rise?

The Smelly Crisps Company has made a large profit this year since it introduced its new brand of sock-flavoured crisps. The board of directors has agreed that some of their staff should get a salary increase to reward them for their work. The problem is that they cannot decide which of four workers should be given the pay rise. They have decided to ask you to help them make this difficult decision.

Paul is a 50-year-old man, married, with two children who are aged 20 and 22. He has worked for the company for thirty years. He is the marketing manager and receives a high salary already. His work is not brilliant but not bad either.

Meena is a 30-year-old woman, married, with one child at nursery. She has worked for the company for five years and does the company accounts. Her salary is high. She often arrives late but her work is brilliant.

Amir is a 22-year-old man, unmarried, with one 5-year-old child. He has worked for the company for two years and it was his idea to produce the new sock-flavoured crisps. His job is to ensure quality control. Recently he has made a bad impression on management by making critical comments. His work is average.

Helen is a 19-year-old woman, unmarried, with one child. She also looks after her ill mother. She has worked for the company for six months, packing the crisp packets into boxes when they come off the conveyer belt. Her work and attendance are poor.

   You must decide which person should get the pay rise and explain why. You should also explain why the others should not be given the pay rise. When you have made a decision, complete the sentences below for each of the 4 people.

.... **should not** be given the pay rise
because ....
....
.... **should not** be given the pay rise
because ....
....
.... **should not** be given the pay rise
because ....
....
.... **should** be given the pay rise
because ....
....

Individual worksheet 11b: Floating and sinking

Pretend there is a tank of water in front of you. Which of the following objects would float and which would sink? Explain the reasoning behind your answers.

	Float	Sink	Because …
A flat metal pencil case will			....
A metal toy truck will			....
A plastic bottle will			....
A plastic ruler will			....
A wooden tray will			....
A wooden chopstick will			....

Worksheet 11c: Floating and sinking

Which objects do you, as a group, think will float? And which do you think will sink? (For each object, go around the group and find out what the pupils wrote when they completed the sheet individually.) Talk about the reasons you gave for your individual predictions and come up with an agreed group prediction, and why you think the objects will float or sink. The scribe should record these below.

We predict that a flat metal pencil case will float/sink because ....

....

....

We predict that a metal toy truck will float/sink because ....

....

....

We predict that a plastic bottle will float/sink because ....

....

....

We predict that a plastic ruler will float/sink because ....

....

....

We predict that a wooden tray will float/sink because ....

....

....

We predict that a wooden chopstick will float/sink because ....

....

....

Roles within group work

UPPER PRIMARY

Resources

Pens, paper, Worksheets 12b and 12c, and Teacher information sheet 12a.

Learning objectives

- To get pupils thinking about the various roles or special jobs they can take on when working in a group
- To get pupils thinking about what different roles might entail
- To get pupils thinking about how they perform different roles
- To give pupils practice in performing roles

Briefing and introduction – whole class work (ten minutes)

Explain that in some group-work activities it is helpful if group members take on special roles to help in accomplishing the task. Discuss the lesson objectives and the following questions:

- What different roles or special jobs might be used during group work?
- What do these roles or special jobs involve?

Here are some suggestions for the roles that might be used most often:

- Chairperson/manager/organiser/coordinator
- Scribe/note-taker/secretary
- Timekeeper
- Supporter/praiser/encourager
- Observer/evaluator
- Spokesperson
- Helper/adviser

There may also be other roles that are particular to the activity: for example, for an activity involving planning a school outing, responsibility for organising transport, organising equipment or picnic-maker.

Remind pupils that a group should use roles only when they are absolutely necessary. Roles such as opinion-seeker, information-giver, ideas person, explanation-seeker, tension-releaser and so on are all roles that all group members should be adopting all the time, and thus do not need to be specifically designated.

It may be that you want to allocate roles to particular pupils so that the group activity involves them more, makes best use of their skills (e.g. to help include a child with SEN), or to ensure that they get practice in other roles.

Group activity – role descriptions (ten to fifteen minutes)

It is important that pupils have a clear sense about what is involved in carrying out the role and also how to take on the role in practice in terms of what might be said and done.

Organise pupils into small groups of three or four. Allocate each group one of four roles to discuss. The group should identify a job description for their role and list this on a single sheet of paper. (Note: these could be referred to by other pupils in the future when taking on that role.) At this point teachers may decide that a debriefing is necessary before ending the lesson or continuing with the remaining tasks which may be best covered on another day.

Preparation for electric circuits/insulators work (five to ten minutes)

Use the same groups as in the previous task. Outline what the groups will have to do in relation to the task below and ask the pupils to come up with some ideas as to how they would perform their role in terms of what they might say and do according to their job descriptions. These could be listed in a 'T' chart on a sheet of paper (see p. 112).

Repeat this exercise prior to doing the tasks on electricity/insulators to identify a different approach to performing the role in a different context.

Group work – electric circuits, conductors and insulators (ten to fifteen minutes)

The objective is to give pupils experience of carrying out their roles in a different type of task. Children should remain in the groups used for the previous discussion task.

Allow pupils five minutes to discuss and plan how they will perform their roles before giving them the materials to start doing their task.

Depending on the previous experience of your class in this area, give pupils either the task of predicting whether the bulb will light up (Worksheet 12b) or the task of predicting whether certain materials act as insulators or conductors (Worksheet 12c).

Debriefing (five to ten minutes)

Discuss pupils' answers and explanations. Ask pupils how they got on with their roles. Identify a few examples of how children carrying out each role put that role into practice. Did they do things differently from in the previous task? What did they say and do? Did they find it difficult to do their role and contribute to the group discussion at the same time? Did anyone find that they could not perform their role because they were too involved in the group discussion? Any thoughts on how they could perform their role better in future?

Follow-up work

Encourage groups to think about whether they need to take on roles, which roles are useful and which they are not good at performing. This could be part of a discussion about how pupils can further improve their group-working skills.

Teacher information sheet 12a: Key to circuitry symbols

1 Battery or cell	
2 Batteries	
Wire	
Lamp	
Closed switch (on)	
Open switch (off)	

Answers to 'Working circuits' diagrams

The bulbs in Diagrams 1, 4 and 6 will be lit. Diagrams 2 and 3 have no battery. In Diagram 5 the switch is off.

Answers to 'Insulators and conductors'

Wood, plastic and rubber all act as insulators. Metal and water conduct electricity.

Worksheet 12b: Working circuits

Look at each of the circuit diagrams. Do you think the bulb(s) are alight?
Complete the sentences by crossing out the answer that is wrong and
writing in the reason for your group answer.

   Make sure you find out what each person in your group thinks. Talk about
your reasons. Make sure you come to an agreed **group** answer and reason
why you think the bulb(s) will be alight or not.

1 We think the bulb is alight/not alight because	
2 We think the bulbs are alight/ not alight because	
3 We think the bulb is alight/not alight because	
4 We think the bulb is alight/not alight because	
5 We think the bulb is alight/not alight because	
6 We think the bulbs are alight/ not alight because	

Worksheet 12c: Insulators and conductors

An easy way to test whether materials are conductors or insulators is to use this circuit.

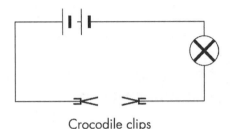

Crocodile clips

Attach the crocodile clips to two different parts of the material. If the bulb lights up then this shows that the material is a conductor. If the bulb does not light up then it is an insulator.

Imagine that you are using this circuit. Which materials do you **as a group** think will act as an insulator and which will act as a conductor?

Make sure you find out what each person in your group thinks. Talk about your reasons. Make sure you come to an agreed **group** prediction and reason why you think the item will act as a conductor or an insulator.

1   We predict that a wooden chopstick will act as a conductor/insulator because

   ....

   ....

2   We predict that a flat metal pencil case will act as a conductor/insulator because

   ....

   ....

3   We predict that a plastic comb will act as a conductor/insulator because

   ....

   ....

4   We predict that a rubber band will act as a conductor/insulator because

   ....

   ....

5   We predict that water in a glass will act as a conductor/insulator because

   ....

   ....

Unit 13

Planning group work

UPPER PRIMARY

Resources

Worksheet 13a, pens, paper and materials for the 'Great gadgets' task.

Learning objectives

- To get pupils thinking about how they can plan and organise themselves and their work during group-work tasks so that they are less reliant on the teacher
- To give pupils practice in planning and organising their group work during different types of task

Briefing – whole class work (ten minutes)

Explain to pupils that they have been doing quite a lot of group work, but that you have often been deciding how the group work should be done, how they should organise themselves and so on. Discuss the above objectives. Explain that they are now going to think together about how they can plan and organise *their own* group work.

Either in the context of an imaginary piece of group work or in terms of preparation for the 'Great gadgets' task, discuss the things pupils will have to think about when planning and organising their own group work so that they can come up with a plan of action. What will they have to think about to prepare for this task? How can they make sure that everyone is involved and contributing efficiently?

Some things to consider doing when planning for group work:

- Timetable – How can they use their time effectively? How much time should they spend doing different jobs? Do they need to evaluate how things are going so that they can change their plan if need be?
- Group roles – Are group roles needed? If so, which ones? (Refer to roles outlined on p. 152.)
- Brainstorming – Will the group need to brainstorm ideas? Will people need some individual thinking time to develop some ideas?

- Decision making – Will the group need to make *joint* decisions?
- Sub-tasks – Can the main task be broken down into smaller tasks? If so, can any of these be done at the same time?
- Sub-groups – For which tasks will the group need to work together to make joint decisions? Can the group split up to do some specific jobs?
- Note-taking/recording – Will a record or minutes be needed?

Briefing – whole class work (five minutes)

Discuss the main objectives for the lesson. Remind pupils about what they did in the last lesson and pick up on some of the ways they went about planning for their paired work. Build a discussion on this and how they could take it forward.

Group work – 'Great gadgets' (twenty minutes)

The idea behind this task is to create an unrealistic time pressure which will persuade groups to break into sub-groups, delegate jobs, identify roles for different sub-tasks and coordinate these sub-groups and sub-tasks.

Split the class into groups of five or six pupils. Outline what they will have to do in the main part of the activity but do not give them any materials to work with. Groups should be given five minutes to plan how they will do their group-work activity and to anticipate any problems. You may then want to have a whole class discussion in which groups outline how they will be organising their group work and possibly adjust their plans.

Groups are to devise a 'great gadget' (see Worksheet 13a) with a catchy name, a billboard poster and a TV commercial to advertise it, possibly featuring a short poem or a jingle. They will have only *fifteen minutes* (or an even less realistic deadline) to complete this task. Give the groups the materials they need to do their tasks:

- Card, paper clips, elastic bands, lolly sticks or pencils, etc. – to build the gadget
- Paper and one pen – to design the billboard poster
- Paper and one pen – to write the TV advert

Remind groups to pay special attention to the practicality, usefulness, sleekness of design and 'saleability' of the gadget. Their gadget will be judged on these criteria by the rest of the class, who will see the gadget, poster and TV advert at the end of the task.

Do not remind pupils that their time is nearly up until they have only a minute to go, since this is the job of a timekeeper. If they run out of time, they could finish their gadgets, posters or adverts at a later point.

Having seen each group's gadget, billboard poster and TV advert, the other groups should provide feedback (positive and negative) and/or rate the work: for example, thumbs up or down from each group on the criteria, such as practicality, usefulness, sleekness of design and 'saleability', to find out which gadget people are most likely to buy.

Debriefing (ten to fifteen minutes)

Discuss with the class how the groups organised their work, possibly using the following questions:

- How did you plan your group work?
- How could you have organised things better?
- Did you use roles?
- Was this helpful and why?
- Could you have performed your role better?
- Did anyone feel they had nothing or little to do?
- How did your group decide what type of gadget to make?
- Did every group member have an opportunity to express an idea or view?
- Did any group split into smaller groups that were given particular jobs?
- Did this work well?
- Did anyone experience a breakdown in coordination between the sub-groups?
- Did any group have any disagreements?
- How did they resolve problems given that there was so little time?

Follow-up work

You may like to set longer-term projects which can be carried out over a few sessions or weeks and involve a number of sub tasks. Encourage groups to plan their group work actively beforehand and to review progress at regular intervals.

Worksheet 13a: Great gadgets

Your group task is going to be to devise a 'great gadget' that can be used in the kitchen, at school, on a building site, in a hospital or anywhere you want. It has to be useful and practical, look good and people must want to buy it. You will also need to create a billboard poster such as you see on the side of roads and an idea for a TV advert with a short poem or jingle to promote your great gadget. Your gadget must have a catchy name.

You will have only a short amount of time to do this task, so you will need to plan how you are going to do the group work. You may not have enough time to do all of the work together. Here are some questions to help you in your planning.

- Will you need to do some brainstorming?
- What decisions will have to be agreed by the whole group?
- Will you need to have group-work roles? Why? Which ones will you need?
- Will you need to split the group into smaller groups to do different parts of the task?
- Do you need to have a timetable?

What is your plan of action?

First we are going to ....

....

Then we will ....

....

Then ....

....

Then ....

....

Then ....

....

Then..

....

- How many minutes will you spend on each task?
- What problems do you think may arise?
- How will you deal with them?

Index